COUNSELLING AS A CAREER

Robert Ross

Cartoons by Kate Cowdy

Cover Illustration by Nick Hedges

Baldrick

First published in 1997 by Baldrick Press, Vine Cottage,
Church Walk, Combe, Witney, Oxon OX8 8NQ
(01993 898430)

ISBN 0 9530477 0 9

Typeset by Connell Publishing, Moreton House, Moreton,
Thame, Oxon, UK
Printed in Britain by Information Press, Southfield Road,
Eynsham, Oxon OX8 1JJ

CONTENTS

Acknowledgements vii

Chapter 1: The Evolution and Growth of Counselling 1

Chapter 2: Training 20

Chapter 3: Counselling in Medical Settings 32

Chapter 4: Work Related Counselling 46

Chapter 5: Counselling in Educational Settings 60

Chapter 6: Counselling in Pastoral Care Settings 73

Chapter 7: Counselling in the Community 85

Chapter 8: Careers Counselling 96

Chapter 9: Counselling in Private Practice 108

Chapter 10: Your Questions Answered 120

Chapter 11: CVs, Applications and Interviews 126

Appendix: Counselling in Sport and Entertainment 139

References and Useful Addresses 146

"With such large numbers of people now taking counselling courses it is essential that they are given a proper idea of what the market is like for counselling jobs, and how they might progress towards the type of counselling work they wish to do. Here is a book which realistically sets out the possibilities, and gives very helpful guidance on how best to take advantage of them." **Michael Jacobs, Fellow of the British Association for Counselling**

"No other volume brings together such relevant comprehensive information about work settings and counselling courses." **Head of Voluntary Counselling Agency**

. . . "well researched, reflects current practice and trends and contains many useful tips as well as valuable background information" . . . **Margaret Dane, President of AGCAS**

"The insights into counselling in sport and entertainment are very revealing" . . . **Prof. Sidney Bloch, author of 'Introduction to the Psychotherapies'**

. . . "The author's wide range of background and experience works to substantiate the sorts of questions about suitability, motivation, capacity and so on that any career seekers must explore in themselves." **Publishing Advisor**

Dedication

To my wife Mary, and my children Stephen and Kirsten

Acknowledgements

I am grateful to Colin Feltham for first suggesting that I should write this book, and also Susan Worsey, for many of their suggestions and guidelines. Margaret Dane and Ben Ball were kind enough to offer encouragement and feedback on the whole draft manuscript, and Tony Watts, Sidney Bloch and Myra Bennett acted as referees at a critical time. Sue Weaver should take much of the credit for Counselling at Work. Individual chapters were much improved by valuable suggestions, additions and feedback from Paul Sheppy, Keith Cooper, Jim Pye, Wyn Bramley, Isobel Palmer, and Ben Ball again. Sue Wilkinson helped keep me going when the project was in danger of stalling. The staff of Ward 6D at the JR2 Hospital, Oxford, and at Grove House, Bristol, also helped me see this book as a very worthwhile project during my health problems. Counselling in medical settings will always have a special resonance for me.

I would like to thank all the counsellors who contributed to my case studies and "days/weeks in the life of". I shall not be in the least bit surprised if these turn out to be the most popular parts of the book, where counselling comes to life. I am also grateful to the BAC for masses of information, and private practitioners who kindly supplied the data for my surveys. I really enjoyed analysing the results.

Thanks are due to John Cleese, Windy Dryden and Sidney Bloch for providing the inspiration for "counselling in sport and entertainment". Strictly for "bon viveurs", I thoroughly enjoyed writing this appendix. If the companion "training video" ever gets produced then thanks are due to Shirley Hill, Sue Weaver, Sue Wilkinson and Andrew Ward for their unforgettable demonstration of counselling techniques. They, and my other colleagues at Oxford Brookes University Careers Centre, gave me a truly memorable and affectionate send up/send off on January 31st 1997.

I am especially grateful to Michael Jacobs for finally convincing me of the overall merits of the manuscript and its marketability. I shall be delighted if Open University Press at some point in the future publish a revised, second edition. I also very much appreciated Alice Meadows' marketing and publicity advice in the face of my erratic ideas and entrepreneurial inexperience, and also Ros Connell's calm and professional approach to production.

This is a rather serious book about a rather serious profession, and so I am deeply grateful to Kate Cowdy for allowing her imagination to run riot with the cartoons, especially the less politically correct ones. Laughter is the best therapy. I also wanted a striking front cover and I am delighted with Nick Hedges' brilliant artwork, at the risk of putting off some readers from pursuing a career in counselling.

Finally I would like to thank my wife Mary, for rescuing the text as and when I pressed the wrong button on the word-processor, keeping my feet on the ground when my head got into the academic clouds, and generally helping me to maintain the healthy scepticism that this baffling career of counselling deserves.

CHAPTER I:
THE EVOLUTION AND GROWTH OF COUNSELLING

"All professions are conspiracies against the laity" (John Betjamin). So why add another one?

Introduction

The growth and development of counselling in Britain in the last thirty five years has been remarkable. This activity, characterised by caring for and helping others, is now on the brink of becoming a profession in its own right. In many hospitals and general practices counsellors have taken their place alongside nurses, clinical psychologists and other established professions as valued members of the health team. Nearly all colleges of further and higher education have counselling services and careers and educational guidance is achieving a much higher profile in the mid 1990s. In the workplace there is widespread agreement that counselling and stress management can play a major role in the health and wellbeing of employees, and not just those who work in the front line of uniformed and emergency services. Counselling has long been established in the Church and now their more senior counsellors are paid and their training courses are becoming more rigorous. Private practice receives referrals from those who practice in medical, work and community settings and is becoming well established in its own right, albeit mostly on a part-time basis. An estimated two million plus jobs in the UK involve some counselling, around 40,000 earn their living from it and a staggering half million do so part-time. Lesley White (1997) put it rather succinctly:–

. . . "To be loved, admired, needed by clients whose numbers never diminish, only grow as the word is spread, is a powerful attraction" . . .

Counselling can be said to have captured the popular imagination, with characters in famous soap operas such as 'Eastenders' and 'The Archers' engaging in counselling. The death of Marge Proops, Britain's most famous agony aunt, gave rise to the comment that we now live in a 'counselling orientated society'. Some are predicting a 'bonanza' for counselling as central government grapples with the problems of inadequate parenting. It is now commonplace for counselling to be offered to distressed survivors, and their families, of traumatic events such as disasters and murders. Along with this media exposure and wider public awareness of 'post traumatic stress disorder' has come the call for more accountability and closer scrutiny of the costs and benefits of counselling. A common criticism is that counselling has 'highjacked' the role traditionally filled by extended family and local community, and the reputation of counselling and therapy has been questioned recently by the publicity surrounding 'false memory syndrome'. White (1997) observed that–

"British culture has absorbed the caring message of counselling like a sponge, used its resonance in education, medicine, entertainment and even flogging phone time – 'It's good to talk.'"

The British Association for Counselling (BAC) is leading the way and there is now a United Kingdom Register of Counsellors (UKRC), the first step towards a recognised profession. The British Confederation of Psychotherapists (BCP) also has a register, as does the British Psychological Society (BPS) for Chartered Counselling Psychologists. European Union regulations allow counsellors from EU countries where there is a national register to practice in the UK, but conversely, prevent counsellors from the UK who are not registered from practicing in Europe. For counselling to grow further and develop it will have to demonstrate that it is worthwhile, good value for money, and responsible in the way it organises, selects and accredits the counsellors.

Who This Book is For?

The obvious place to debate the issues raised in this book is in the final term of the final year of advanced counselling diploma courses, the very time when many will be applying for perhaps their first professional counselling post. They will have obtained supervised counselling experience, and will probably have also done voluntary work. However, I would like to think that students at foundation and certificate levels will find the book helpful in their decision whether or not to take their training further. For long term professional accreditation and development, counsellors will be in and out of 'college' throughout their working lives.

Many nurses, teachers, social workers, human resource managers, clergy, and careers guidance workers will be contemplating the possibility in specialising in counselling and hence a career change. Even lawyers, police officers, advice workers and others may find themselves so taken by the use of counselling skills in their work as to contemplate change, at least at a part-time level. Many busy professionals, especially women, are questioning their overall quality of life as they work their average 44 hours per week (the highest in Europe), often under stress. 'Downshifting', a choice to work less and embrace a better balanced, richer (though less well-off) lifestyle, is becoming increasingly popular, and a part-time career in counselling may play its part. Not that counselling is stress free: far from it, but it can be engaged in moderation. The choice is yours, especially as counselling lends itself to flexitime, part-time, job-sharing etc.

What is Counselling?

According to the BAC counselling occurs when:–

"a counsellor sees a client in a private and confidential setting to explore a difficulty the client is having, distress they may be experiencing, or perhaps their dissatisfaction with life or loss of a sense of direction and purpose. It is always at the request of the client" . . . (BAC 1996, Information Sheet 10)

Richard Nelson-Jones (1991) also describes counselling as a helping relationship and he identifies counselling services as catering for the needs of the relatively less disturbed. He therefore draws the distinction from seriously disturbed people who would normally be treated by a psychiatrist (eg. for psychosis), or a clinical psychologist (eg. for phobias). Colin Feltham (1995) provides an even handed and highly readable account of definitions of counselling/psychotherapy including, at the heroic end of the scale, 'urgent and pragmatic responses to human suffering', and 'a relationship that is experienced as healing'. Lending an air of mystery is the notion of a 'loving, listening kind of guesswork', whereas various sceptics and critics have concluded that it is 'amateurish, well-meaning do-goodery'. In his Forward to Feltham's book Alvin Mahler argues that:–

. . . "there are probably more differences among its (counselling) graduates than there are between its graduates and the graduates of those trained in any of the other professions that train counsellors or psychotherapists . . . Such a profession does not exist." (p vii)

Wyn Bramley (1996) too highlights the mysterious nature of the work:

. . . "The therapist uses her ideas (unprovable) to guide her feelings (untestable) about the process (invisible) to guide her towards interpretations (debatable) of what might 'really' (whose reality?) be happening. Small wonder that much of the general public regard our profession with suspicion!" (p 12)

Some psychologists such as Gale (1990) appear less than impressed with counsellors who offer professional help but lack 'special expertise'. Perhaps it is because some of the work is unpaid and much of the training is introductory level that some psychotherapists and psychologists wish to distance themselves from counselling. At worst counselling/psychotherapy will be equated with brainwashing and cult phenomena and Naylor-Smith (1994) offers a timely reminder of the need for caution:–

"Any client/practitioner relationship has potential for good and for evil. The more intense that relationship is, the greater is the potential for good but also for harm . . . The exploring of the unconscious involves great skill."

Many counsellors discover counselling because of their own experience of severe distress, and very often they have been pursuing careers which contain a counselling dimension such as nursing, social work and teaching. Although counselling is potentially extremely rewarding, the work is difficult and can be stressful (Dryden 1995) and it is an essential requirement that trainees are psychologically healthy enough to bear the strain. BAC now require 40 hours of personal counselling towards accreditation. Once you have decided that you have the potential, emotional stability and serious interest to become a counsellor you might want to address the following questions. With which client groups and range of issues do you want to work, in which settings, and on which model or models of counselling would your practice be based?

Models

The boundaries of counselling and psychotherapy are hard to define and have been the subject of much controversy. For example Jennifer Elton-Wilson (1994) argues that many psychotherapists aim to provide for their clients a more fundamental change of character and personality. However, I agree with Feltham (1995) who concludes that apart from differences in style, with their implicit underlying beliefs, there are no essential differences between the work of counsellors and psychotherapists. He goes on to suggest that in terms of effectiveness there is little if any evidence between the different models of counselling/psychotherapy, although each and every one of them have their devotees. It is important for counsellors to discover which model is going to be most effective for *them* as practitioners, for their particular clients, in their particular settings. There are over 400 different theoretical approaches to counselling and psychotherapy but there are three main groups:- psychoanalytic, which is primarily based upon working with the unconscious, cognitive-behavioural, which focuses on how we think and behave, and humanistic, which espouses an innate potential for self-realization. Of the psychoanalytic and humanistic therapies psychodynamic counselling and person centred counselling respectively are the most commonly practiced in the UK, and two other humanistic therapies which are well established are Gestalt and Transactional Analysis.

Psychodynamic counselling is based on the belief that personal problems are invariably underpinned by hidden (ie unconscious) powerful forces requiring identification, containment, interpretation and working through. The counsellor may be regarded as an expert code-breaker of unconscious messages and it naturally follows that an important element of training is personal therapy. This could last in the region of six to 18 months and cost £500 to £1500. The approach is ideally suited to clients who accept that their problems may be deeply rooted but it has also been adapted to short term work. Psychodynamic counselling is very widely practiced especially in private practice.

At the core of cognitive-behavioural counselling is the observation that our thoughts can be identified and changed, and that behaviour can be profitably experimented with through homework exercises. This approach is often thought to be particularly successful with phobias, compulsions and obsessions, when other talking methods fail or seem to have only a moderate impact. This contrasts sharply with psychodynamic approaches which question the merits of treating merely 'symptoms'. The counsellor can be more directive and might, for example, suggest assignments in which the client experiments with new ways of thinking, acting and coping. The approach is popular with psychologists and is very common in educational, work, and medical settings.

The person-centred approach, widely taught (especially for its basic counselling conditions) on counselling training courses in Britain, argues that human beings are self-directed, creative, positive beings who have their own sense of inner self-worth. These qualities are prevented from flourishing by early adverse life conditions, but they can be nurtured back into health given the core conditions of empathy, unconditional positive regard and genuineness. As Feltham (1995) has stressed, the approach has an in-built anti-authoritarian value system: only the individual knows what he or she needs and no one else has any right to dictate otherwise. Counsellor and client meet as equals and the approach has an optimistic view of human beings, plus an aura of goodness and simplicity, which may explain its attraction. In its purest form, like psychodynamic counselling, it is a long term form of therapy and is very widely practiced especially in pastoral care, community and educational settings.

Of the numerous other humanistic models Transactional Analysis (TA) and Gestalt are probably the most widely taught and practiced. TA contains a relatively simple map of human functioning including the Parent-Adult- Child model, popularised by Eric Berne's 'Games People Play'. Gestalt is a holistic approach co-founded by Fritz Perls as a third force against psychoanalysis and behaviour therapy. According to Feltham (1995) it is dedicated to individualism and a particular kind of spontaneous and expressive individualism at that.

My own counselling practice was rooted in the person centred approach but was modified and developed firstly by Gestalt and later cognitive-behavioural. I doubt that I could have successfully trained to be a psychoanalytic psychotherapist, and, much as I admired him, I was not Carl Rogers (the guru of person centred counselling). As a student counsellor around 90% of my clients were seen for less than four sessions and initially this came to me as a surprise. This compares with BAC members in private practice who might see a client on average for about 12 sessions, whereas the norm for counselling in medical (general practice) settings is around six sessions. Because they often see their work as primarily with the unconscious, 12 sessions would be seen as very brief by many psychotherapists.

However, it is becoming obvious that many counsellors, no doubt keen to discover how best to adapt their own unique personalities to the mysteries of the counselling relationship, will adopt and adapt a combination of two or more models, and Feltham points out that, at least in America, integrative and eclectic approaches are in the ascendant along with cognitive-behavioural. What is true of all counselling approaches is that they are 'talking cures': the client is helped by the unique relationship that is built up with their counsellor. There will always remain in my view some mystery as to how it works, when it works, which is not every time. Except in the private sector long term individual counselling will only ever be available to a minority of clients, and so much interest and research effort is currently focused on time limited approaches Feltham (1996).

Clients and Settings

Most counsellors have to cope with a wide range of both clients and presenting concerns and therefore broadly based training and experience is to be recommended The setting can give some clues as to the types of client and presenting concern, and the appropriateness of different models.

i **Medical**: Especially the elderly, with particular concerns including coping with illness and managing without drugs. Colleagues for obvious reasons will tend to subscribe to 'medical' models of physical and mental illness.

ii **Education**: Students and trainees increasingly come from a wide range of ages and backgrounds but are still predominantly young and academically able. Concerns include anxiety and depression, job prospects, finance, and broken relationships.

iii **Work**: Concerns including stress, redundancy, and issues likely to affect their attendance and effectiveness at work such as illness, bereavement and divorce. Brief work may predominate.

iv **Pastoral Care**: Many clients will hold religious beliefs or experience problems with meaning and perhaps moral decisions. Bereavement and coping with illness will be common concerns.

v **Private Practice**: Clients tend to be middle class and, with sufficient income, there is more scope for long term work.

All counsellors, however, have to be prepared for the unexpected and for many one of the attractions of the work is that no two clients are the same. A counsellor may have to respond creatively, pragmatically and empathically to all kinds of human suffering. Steps you might take towards deciding on your training and practice goals, especially for working in the community, include:—

    i   Be ruthlessly honest about the client groups you would prefer and prefer *not* to work with.

    ii Join a therapy group, or enter counselling yourself as a choice.

    iii Interview practitioners about their methods, client groups and patterns of presenting concerns.

    iv Acknowledge that clients are harder to help (and possibly harder to like) when they are most different from you in terms of culture, age etc.

If you have still to choose your degree course I have no hesitation in recommending psychology and in particular a study programme which meets British Psychological Society (BPS) requirements. However, you should bear in mind that these courses are usually scientific in orientation with subjects like statistics to master, and some lecturers may have little interest in or sympathy for counselling. Other related degree subjects include English literature, theology, philosophy, anthropology and sociology. The most progressive British universities such as Oxford Brookes offer tremendous flexibility of subject choice, change and detailed programme, including BPS accreditation.

Too keen to give advice?

Am I Suited to Counselling?

Answer the following questions quickly and truthfully. Tick one box per question:–

1) When asked for your general advice, how keen are you to give it?
  a) very keen
  b) keen
  c) fairly keen
  d) reluctant
  e) v. reluctant

2) How are you most likely to respond if a client (same sex) appears to fall in love with you?
  a) with horror
  b) with dismay
  c) with fascination
  d) perceive therapeutic opportunity
  e) reciprocate if possible

3) As a fully qualified eclectic counsellor, which approach would you adopt for the following clients?
  i) Basil Fawlty (of 'Fawlty Towers')
    a) person-centred
    b) psychodynamic
    c) cognitive-behavioural
    d) other (specify)
  ii) Victor Meldrew (of 'One Foot in the Grave')
    a) person-centred
    b) psychodynamic
    c) cognitive-behavioural
    d) other (specify)
  iii) Hyacinth Bucket (of 'Keeping Up Appearances')
    a) person-centred
    b) psychodynamic
    c) cognitive-behavioural
    d) other (specify)
  iv) Lord Blackadder (1558-1603)
    a) person-centred
    b) psychodynamic
    c) cognitive-behavioural
    d) other (specify)

4) On an average day how neurotic are you?
  a) very
  b) fairly
  c) slightly
  d) not at all

5) What course of action would you encourage the following clients to take?

i) Manuel (Spanish waiter in 'Fawlty Towers')
   a) return to Spain
   b) change hotels
   c) hit back
   d) counselling
   e) other (specify)

ii) Mrs Meldrew
   a) divorce
   b) separation
   c) euthanasia
   d) counselling
   e) other (specify)

iii) Mr Bucket
   a) divorce
   b) separation
   c) euthanasia
   d) counselling
   e) other (specify)

iv) Baldrick (Lord Blackadder's servant)
   a) join the army
   b) change masters
   c) murder
   d) counselling
   e) other (specify)

6) How prepared are you to work voluntarily?
a) totally
b) keen
c) fairly keen
d) if necessary
e) not

7) Assess your ability to see the world through the following clients' eyes?

i) Alf Garnet (of 'Till Death Us Do Part')
   a) no problem
   b) fairly able
   c) difficult
   d) impossible

ii) Patsy (Joanna Lumley character in 'Absolutely Fabulous')
   a) no problem
   b) fairly able
   c) difficult
   d) impossible

iii) Pamela Anderson's 'Baywatch' Girl
  a) no problem
  b) fairly able
  c) difficult
  d) impossible

8) How much are you (or your partner) prepared to spend on counselling training?
a) £10,000+
b) £5k-10k
c) £2k-5k
d) 0-£2k

For the answers and scores for this quiz turn to the end of this chapter.

The above 'clients' could prove to be quite a test of your aptitude for the 'core conditions' for person-centred counselling: ie how easy is it for you to display accurate empathy, unconditional positive regard and genuineness. In practice the person specification for a counselling job will cover three main areas:–
  i   Knowledge (and understanding) of clients and presenting concerns.
  ii Skills (and abilities, competences, aptitudes) such as listening and empathic responding.
  iii Values (and attitudes) such as support for equal opportunities.

"Listening and emphatic responding"

All these will be reflected in your life and work experience and selection procedures for counselling jobs are primarily designed to ascertain the quality and depth of that experience. Perhaps the most valuable skill in applications and interviews is to demonstrate the *relevance* of your own experience (see chapter 11) which can include paid work, unpaid work and even hobbies. Paper qualifications are a convenient shorthand for established combinations of knowledge and skills and to a lesser extent values, and a degree and/or a professional qualification will most likely be required for good jobs in counselling. Feltham (1995), however, does not think qualifications are everything:–

"I believe that the popular success of counselling in recent years highlights the embarrassing probability that 'lay' people with only a certain amount of training quite possibly often can achieve results similar to those achieved by others who have had expensive and extensive, supposedly specialized training."

Finally, my checklist of the ideal attributes for counsellor would be: Assertive; Believes in life-long training and personal development; Caring; Emotionally stable; Good listener; Impervious to unjustified criticism; Intelligent; Broad and open-minded; Patient; Sensitive; Tolerant. However, you do not have to be Superman or Wonderwoman. Counsellors are human too!

Towards a Profession

Since 1992 many discussions have taken place concerning the possibility of setting up a single, national recognised system for professional self regulation (Thoburn 1995) and this great debate has resulted in the creation of the UK Register of Counsellors and Counselling Organisations (UKRC). It was launched in the summer of 1996 and there are two access routes:–

    i   Individuals who are deemed capable of working as independent practitioners.

    ii Through sponsoring organisations where the individual is registered specifically to work in that organisation.

At present COSCA (Confederation of Scottish Counselling Agencies) is the only other accreditation scheme accepted. This can be seen as a major move towards the establishment of a counselling profession which, at best, would be as inclusive as possible, whilst setting standards for safe and competent practice in which the public and the profession can have confidence. There are 16 criteria for acceptance as a counsellor registered by a sponsoring organisation, and the criteria for independent practitioners are British Association for Counselling accreditation and COSCA individual accreditation. BAC, founded in 1977, is the main national membership body for counselling and its code of ethics and practice is designed to establish and maintain standards for practitioners and to protect members of the public seeking and using their services. Members can join one or more of the BAC Divisions which represent different areas of counselling:–

    APCC   Association for Pastoral Care and Counselling

    ASC   Association for Student Counselling

    ACW   Association for Counselling at Work

CIE   Counselling in Education
CMS   Counselling in Medical Settings
PSRF   Personal/Sexual/Relationship/Family
RACE   Race and Cultural Education in Counselling

The growth of counselling has been phenomenal with the number of counsellors appearing in the British Association for Counselling Directory rising from 127 in 1979/80 to over 2000 in 1996. These tend to be counsellors working at least part time in private practice. The grand total of all members of the BAC was over 15,000 in 1996 and BAC's own survey (1993) showed the following information about this wider membership:—

1 The age range was 26 to 61 plus, with 45% aged 41–50.
2 49% resided in the South-East (30% of UK population).
3 73% were married or cohabiting.
4 Most members had a substantial secondary (non-counselling) activity, for example teaching, welfare advice, administration.
5 63% of members were graduate and of these 26% had Masters degrees.
6 87% had formal counselling qualifications and 86% of these were trained part-time. 92% of members trained part-time spent an average of 2.5 years in their original training. Typically this involved 250–500 hours on courses.
7 Only 26% of members preferred one theoretical counselling model and 12% had two or three. The most frequently mentioned included psychodynamic (60%), person-centred (57%), eclectic (32%), transactional analysis (24%) and cognitive (19%).
8 87% had divisional membership:- Personal/Sexual/Relationship/Family (25%), Student (20%), Medical (20%), Pastoral Care (15%), Work (15%), Education (10%) and Race (4%).

My own 1995 sample survey of 100 listed BAC members showed that 60% were earning less than £10,000 pa from counselling and even full time counselling earnings averaged only £17,500. Of course many of these counsellors had other part time jobs and 75% had the security of salaried partners. Less than half expected their counselling work to grow in the second half of the 1990s and several commented on the growing competition for jobs and clients arising directly from the excessive growth of training courses. On the other hand there are many secure and established counselling jobs, especially in medical and education settings, although the salaries are moderate by professional standards (mostly in the range £15k-22k full time equivalent). Whilst there are some lingering doubts about earning a living, counselling presents a challenging and potentially richly rewarding activity.

To Join the Club?

Would you join a club that would have Bernard Manning as a member? Last year Bernard Manning, the allegedly racist comedian, deeply embarrassed the BAC by presenting himself successfully for membership as a counsellor specialising in racial awareness. I have some sympathy here with the BAC because membership, whilst asking you to subscribe to a code of Ethics and Practice, is not a qualification. I believe BAC have reviewed their procedures and their new UK Register of Counsellors, started in September 1996, is the reliable guide to professionalism through its rigorous system of accreditation.

There are three routes to BAC individual accreditation:–

i Has completed a BAC Recognised Counsellor Training Course *and* has had at least 450 hours of supervised counselling practice. Has undertaken a total of 450 hours of counselling training comprising two elements: (a) 200 hours of skill development and (b) 250 hours of theory and has at least 450 hours of counselling supervised practice over a minimum period of three years; or

ii Can provide evidence of seven years experience in counselling with a minimum of 150 supervised practice hours per year, and has had at least 450 hours of supervised counselling practice over three years; or

iii Can provide evidence of a combination of (a) some formal counselling training and (b) at least 450 hours of supervised practice over three years, and (c) 40 hours of personal therapy.

75 hours of counselling practice = 1 unit.

1 year of supervised practice = 1 unit. Together the total must add up to 10 units.

An applicant is also required to meet the following criteria:–

• Has an agreed formal supervision arrangement of at least one and a half hours per month.
• Gives evidence of serious commitment to ongoing professional and personal development.
• Is a current individual member of BAC.
• Has a philosophy of counselling which includes evidence of at least one theoretical model.
• Demonstrates practice which adheres to the BAC Code of Ethics and Practice for Counsellors.
• Undertake a minimum of 40 hours of personal therapy.

One of the main advantage of membership of BAC is entitlement to be listed in the BAC Counselling and Psychotherapy Resources Directory which is one of the three main sources of client referral for counsellors in private practice. Alternatively membership of the Institute for Psychosexual Medicine or United Kingdom Council for Psychotherapy will entitle listing. The UKCP does for organisations in psychotherapy what BAC does for counselling. The British Psychological Society (BPS) regulates the activities of chartered psychologists for which the relevant divisions are clinical and counselling psychology respectively. If you accept the premise that counselling should become an established profession then accredited membership should be your goal and there is no doubt in my mind that the best counselling jobs will soon require accreditation.

Paid or Unpaid Work?

Hopson and Scally (1984: 27) describe 'work' as

. . . "an activity that can provide us with a sense of purpose and direction, a structure for living, a personal sense of identity and self-respect, companions and friends, and it can influence how other people see us . . . work can, in addition, provide us with money if someone wants to buy what we can do. Whilst there may be a shortage of jobs there will never be a shortage of work."

The established counselling voluntary sector, which is comprehensively analysed by Tyndall (1995), includes:—

Concern	Organisation
Relationships	Relate
Bereavement	Cruse
Victims of Rape	Rape Crisis
Victims of Crime	Victim Support
Mental Illness	MIND

There is also a multiplicity of telephone help lines such as Samaritans and Childline and self help groups usually devoted to single issues such as eating disorder, supporting the relatives of schizophrenics etc. These are too numerous to mention here but they all do valuable work nearly all of which is unpaid. Many voluntary organisations have salaried staff in senior positions and are heavily committed to high standards of training at foundation and certificate levels. A sustained spell of voluntary counselling and commitment to at least certificate level of training will demonstrate the seriousness of your interest in counselling as a career.

Alternatives to Counselling

Psychotherapy is the obvious career choice for budding counsellors who are drawn by head and especially heart to work in depth and long term with people. Jennifer Elton-Wilson (1994) has noted a tendency for some psychotherapists to attempt to maintain an elite position, which differentiates psychotherapy from counselling whilst adopting the mantle of teachers of counselling practice. I do not accept that counselling is in any way second rate when compared to psychotherapy.

Another potential elite are the **counselling psychologists** as their qualifications and professional status arise from no less than six years of study and supervised practice to masters level. However, it is the **clinical psychologist** who is built into the NHS and to a lesser extent other settings and it remains to be seen how the newer counselling division of the BPS will establish itself. BPS publicity (Watts and Bor 1995) talks optimistically but vaguely about counselling psychologists working *alongside others* in a variety of settings including primary health care, business, local counselling centres, academic institutions and private practice. It is, however, the second largest BPS Division.

Psychoanalysis.— There are two very distinctive features of this particularly specialised form of therapy. Firstly, the main element of training is itself being a client (analysand) for years, and, secondly, training takes place largely outside further and higher education. Bramley (1996) points out that proper psychoanalytic technique takes as long as it takes and the attitude is one of sphynx-like inscrutability (the so-called 'blank screen'). By comparison counselling or psychotherapy has to be adapted and modified, especially in the public sector, to meet the constraints of financial, political and institutional reality.

Social work (especially the psychiatric specialism), **nursing** (especially psychiatric) and **occupational therapy** are all caring professions from which specialization into counselling is possible. The shift required of practitioners is largely a psychological one given the tremendous emphasis on *non-directive* methods of working in counselling. Many counselling trainees confirm how hard it is to avoid *leading the client* (a cardinal sin!) which is precisely what they have often been doing as social workers, nurses and so on with clients whose self-destructive behaviour may sometimes seem obvious. A useful way of learning more about these counselling related professions is to work for a spell as a nursing auxiliary, OT aide, or volunteer in welfare advice. This will no doubt give you insight into your preferences of working with different client groups including the seriously disadvantaged. **Teaching** and the **ministry** are also caring professions with established training routes into the career of counselling.

Human resources management (or personnel management) is not a caring profession as such although this is a common misunderstanding by candidates who want 'to work with people'. However, it is possible to train further and specialise to the extent of becoming an employee counsellor although much of this work is contracted out to the private sector. The recent merger between the Institutions of Personnel Management and Training and Development is symbolic of the integrated ways which organisations are increasingly adopting in relation to considering the needs and potentials of their workforce.

Careers guidance is well established in localities, further and higher education, with the primary role to provide *counselling*, advice and information through individual interviews and work with groups (Riddick, Ross and McIntyre 1996). Some practitioners within the Central Government Department of Employment work as employment advisers *counselling* unemployed people under the RESTART scheme. Such staff may possess a wide variety of qualifications not necessarily including counselling or a degree. **Educational guidance** for adults includes counselling as one of nine areas but the client centred nature of educational guidance services is paramount. Most graduate entrants have a postgraduate qualification such as teaching, careers, or counselling.

Advice work where counselling skills may be extensively used include Citizens Advice Bureaux, Disablement Information and Advice Line (DIAL), dealing with problems and queries from disabled people, Student Advice which covers welfare issues (e.g. grants, benefit entitlement) and may be tailored to particular groups (e.g. Mature Access Course Students). Riddick et al (1996) point out that advice workers do not normally have the training or resources to act as counsellors in the fuller sense.

Counselling skills are used in all the above careers and also in other professions that deal with people in trouble or distress such as solicitor, prison governor and police officer. There is a significant difference between counselling skills training, which is designed to enhance your performance in your current work, and counselling as a career where the expertise is extremely subtle and advanced training is to be recommended.

The Changing Pattern of Work and Careers

In order to understand the trends and forecasts of the counselling profession it is useful to look at the broader employment picture in the UK. Rajan (1992) identifies nine key trends of which several have implications for the career of counselling.

1 The skills content of work will increase in many occupations.

2 Demographic changes include an ageing population and more women at work. Careers and educational guidance will be sought from a more diverse age range.

3 Unemployment will remain high (over 5%).

4 Employers will convert their standardised products and services into customised ones.

5 Many organisations are unbundling themselves into a collection of smaller units and an increasing proportion of the UK workforce will be either self-employed or work in small and medium sized units.

6 Employees fall into three groups. Firstly sustenance-driven (cautious, prefer status quo and predictability), secondly outer-directed (ambitious, materialistic) and thirdly inner-directed, the group that will become the dominant group in shaping the future. These individuals set most store by personal development and care little for temporary fashion.

7 Organisational changes will involve networking, team-working, flatter structures and shorter hierarchies. There has been a growing decentralisation of work and loose networks will increasingly prevail, with an individual working in different ad-hoc teams or task forces.

Counsellors have the skills and potential to play a major role working with individuals and small groups both within organisations and private practice. The opportunities for women may be especially bright because of their alleged preference and aptitude for teamworking. Counselling is, arguably, a 'feminine' occupation.

One in three school leavers are now expected to enter higher education and women are taking more advantage of the huge expansion in higher education than men. A rapidly increasing proportion of high flyers are mature students such as women returning after raising a family and maturity, of course, is a major asset in counselling training as is the experience of parenting. Until equal opportunities legislation 20 years ago relatively few women were encouraged or enabled to go to university and this helps to explain why so many excellent older counsellors do not have formal qualifications such as a degree. Of course, I am not suggesting that you have to be a graduate but I do reckon that professional counselling posts will increasingly go to well educated and well qualified candidates.

The top growth subject area in higher education is 'allied to medicine'. Psychology, the discipline that most underpins counselling, is emerging as one of the most popular subjects of the 1990s and is expected to grow very rapidly regardless of related job prospects. Most of the growth in jobs up to the year 2000 will be in knowledge-based and skill-intensive occupations but The Central Services Unit (1994) notes, however, that graduate supply increasingly outstrips demand. Two significant changes in recruitment methods are identified: firstly rising entry standards and, secondly, restricting advertisements. This suggests that qualifications up to post graduate standard and creative job search techniques are becoming increasingly important.

The Jobs and the Training

I analysed nearly 200 mostly full time jobs advertised in mid 1994 in BAC Jobfile (a vacancy bulletin for subscribers) with a salary range of £11,000–£31,000 pa (full time equivalent). Interestingly the overall median salary of £17,500 coincided exactly with the average income of a full time counsellor in private practice (estimated from another of my own sample surveys) but of course the latter do not enjoy the additional benefits of working for an organisation such as paid holidays, sickness benefit etc. Salaries tended to be higher in the private and university sectors. I also noticed a bewildering array of named client groups such as dangerous adolescent boys, Asian students, chronic pain sufferers and their families, and aid workers returning from war zones. This reminds me of the amazing variety of professional counselling work to be done and of the need to give careful consideration to your profile of related life and work experience.

A typical full time job will involve 20–30 hours per week working with individuals and small groups, with the rest of the time made up of administration, meetings, reading, training and supervision. The level of training required may be the equivalent of at least one year of full time postgraduate counselling education. Organisations, especially in the public sector, may welcome applications from job-share partners and legislation in 1996 has strengthened the position of part time employees. But temporary and short term contracts are becoming the norm and this is reflected in my own recent experience. After nearly three decades of four different, secure, full time, public sector careers I worked for three years on part time 12 month contracts for a university that increasingly operated as if it was in the private sector: I also did occasional consultancy work in ad-hoc teams. Following final retirement I am working as a free-lance careers consultant, author and playwright.

My own sample of counselling jobs advertised in 1995 showed an average of 20 applicants for each job but around 25% of these actually failed to meet the minimum requirements. My own experience of interviews, and all the other final selection elements, suggests that around one half of the shortlisted candidates perform disappointingly. The lesson is clear: there might be strong competition for counselling jobs but with sound preparation you are in with a good chance.

The only way to improve the long term security of your counselling work is to be demonstrably good at it. I was not surprised to discover in another of my own surveys that recommendation by current or former clients is one of the three major sources of clients for counsellors in private practice. Self employed counsellors have to balance the attraction of autonomy with the inherent insecurity. There are delights of working from home but there are also costs and other potential disadvantages which have led some private practitioners to rent a room in a suitable building.

The sources of information about the counselling scene in *your* locality include the BAC Resources Directory and Yellow Pages (under 'Counselling and Advice', 'Psychotherapy and Analysis', 'Therapists', and 'Hypnotherapists') which list for potential clients a bewildering array of helpers. There may be little overlap between the BAC Directory and Yellow Pages in terms of counselling practice and it may well be that those who aspire to counselling as an established and recognised *profession* belong to the former group. In my own locality I note that the most common concerns in addition to 'general' for which counselling is offered include relationships, substance abuse, bereavement, depression, careers and stress. Your county council social services department will have information about voluntary work opportunities and the BAC Training Directory will list local courses. The best known and established counsellors may well have waiting lists for clients, may *not* advertise, and they will probably be acting as supervisors to counsellors in organisations and private practice. You may find it helpful to track them down and pick their brains.

12 Ways of Getting In and Getting On

1 Do voluntary work.

2 Join the nearest counselling/psychotherapy society; get to know people, especially influential people such as established supervisors.

3 Design different versions of your CV. Whilst the bare facts remain the same (e.g. employed by . . .) highlighting particular client groups (e.g. ethnic minority students) and relevant experiences (e.g. students struggling with illness) will bring out your versatility.

4 Sample survey private practitioners to identify the most helpful supervisor for your own work. Ideally she or he is highly regarded, has a waiting list of clients (and hence refers to her supervisees), is involved in training, and is approaching retirement.

5 Approach potential employers direct and offer, as appropriate, to work temporarily to cover for maternity leave, illness, holidays, extra busy periods etc, perhaps for no pay for a trial period.

6 Subscribe to BAC Jobfile. Note the patterns of vacancies and deduce what might be the equivalent versions in your locality (unadvertised?).

7 Arrange to interview key personnel, ie those who know when vacancies and related opportunities are likely to arise. They include personnel managers in large organisations, directors of student services departments, advanced counselling course leaders, independent counselling centre managers, EAP directors.

9 Arrange to job shadow someone currently doing the very job you most want. Volunteer to help out.

10 Collect all plaudits (e.g. thank you letters for your contributions) for subsequent use in your CV.

11 Identify the largest general practices that do not have a practice counsellor.

12 Start small and plan big. Don't be shy. Actions speak louder than words.

Conclusions

Counselling is a baffling, intriguing, frustrating, challenging, useful, and potentially rewarding career. Only rarely will it be your first job and you are likely to move progressively into it via the combination of caring employment, voluntary work and your own experience as a client. Counselling is also atypical in that much of the work is unpaid and/or part-time. It is easily confused with giving advice and is sometimes indistinguishable from psychotherapy. Counselling is well established as a significant element of the work of social workers, teachers and other professionals, but is increasingly taking on the character of a profession, with recognised courses, a code of ethics and so on. The strategy you need in order to make a start or further develop your counselling career will hinge on obtaining the right kind of both training and experience. It is never too late to start but you will probably have to pay for your training, your own therapy and also work sometimes without pay. The right qualifications will not be enough and you will need to polish your skills of both written and oral communication to be offered a well paid counselling job. If your main aim is to work in private practice it is going to take both time and networking to build up your client base. This is just a brief summary of the position: the chapters that follow describe in more detail how training will further your quest to become a counsellor, and the different areas in which you may choose to seek work.

Am I Suited to Counselling? Answers to the Quiz

1) a 0; b -1; c 2; d 2; e 1
2) a -1; b 0; c 1; d 2; e -2
3) i) a 1; b 0; c -1; d 2(G)
ii) a 0; b 0; c 1; d 2
iii) a 1; b 1; c 1; d 2(TA)
iv) a 1; b 1; c 0; d 2(A)
4) a -2; b -1; c 2; d 1
5) i) a -1; b 2; c 1; d -2; e <2*
ii) a -2; b -2; c -2; d 2; e <2*
iii) a -2; b -2; c -2; d 1; e <2*
6) a 1; b 1; c 2; d -1; e -2
7) i) a 1; b 2; c -1; d -2
ii) a 1; b 2; c -1; d -2
ii) a 1; b 2; c -1; d -2
iii) a 1; b 2; c -1; d -2
8) a <2; b <2; c <2; d <2

*Score up to two points for alternative, ingenious solutions.
G – Gestalt. TA – Transactional Analysis. A – Analysis.

1) Giving Advice. Students on pure person centred training courses (and some tutors) tend to get paranoid about this. Experienced practitioners tend to be more relaxed and can monitor any unhealthy client dependence.
2) Loving is an occupational hazard: learn how to handle it. A good topic for supervision.
3) i) Gestalt. You can be creative without serious risk of offending. Possible referral for psychiatry.
ii) No action required. Victor is basically happy as he is and will live to a ripe old age.
iii) Transactional Analysis. Make sure Hyacinth does not draw you into any games. eg "If it weren't for you".
iv) Analysis. Blackadder can afford it and will enjoy doing all the talking. Keep interpretations to a minimum.

4 Very mild neurosis is, arguably, the normal human condition and enables you to identify with clients. Really well adjusted people should perhaps aim for alternative careers such as hospital manager or politician.

5 i d) Score one point if you speak excellent Spanish.

iii d) The case for counselling is unclear: after all Mr B tends to ignore her.

iv No fee for counselling Baldrick. Two points for helping him with his 'cunning plans' because he is very creative inspite of being very thick.

6 This scoring system is designed for a professionally ambitious student at advanced diploma level. Adjust your score according to the sliding scale you would charge clients in your own private practice.

7 With the possible exception of Carl Rogers and Lucie Loquette (appendix I) some clients are hard to like or understand. However, we should be able, when necessary, to tap into the darker recesses of our own personalities (zenophobia, substance abuse, bimbo etc)

8 a) and b) score two if your ambition is full time professional counselling. If you are not prepared to invest any money at all then stop reading this book now and do something more useful.

Some clients are hard to like

Your score:—

30 You cheated; unsuitable for counselling.

20+ Go ahead with your counselling training.

15–20 Review your strengths and weaknesses, preferably with a careers counsellor.

10–15 Challenge this scoring system: think carefully about which type of therapy suits you best.

<10 Don't give up the day job. Perhaps you are better suited to being a client than a counsellor.

CHAPTER 2:
TRAINING

Introduction

Much to the dismay of those who want to see counselling as a recognised profession or at the very least see some safeguards for clients, anyone can set themselves up as a counsellor or psychotherapist. Perhaps because of the strong traditions of voluntary counselling for organisations such as Relate and Samaritons, counselling even with appropriate training is not necessarily seen as a professional activity. This situation has been further confused by the introduction of unpaid counsellors in some new settings to work alongside established professions. However, it is now extremely unlikely that you will get a counselling job without the appropriate training and qualifications and all the indicators are that counselling, with the notable exception of those BAC accredited by the 'grandparent' route, is becoming an all graduate profession.

I do not mean that employers of counsellors will expect all candidates to have completed degrees and neither do I mean that students of advanced counselling must all be graduates. Women in their forties and fifties are especially likely to be interested in counselling as a career, but before 1975 they were routinely discriminated against in both employment and training and for that, and other cultural factors, were therefore far less likely to go to college. Of course, some of these become in time very successful mature students and the age of mass higher education is upon us now with more female students than male. However, it is reasonable for advanced course leaders, in the absence of a degree or equivalent professional qualification, to expect high standards of life and work experience because counselling is a demanding career. Unqualified and under-qualified people can and do cause harm, and if you are very neurotic then no amount of training will equip you adequately for the task.

Unsuitable for training . . . "pull yourself together"

A Hierarchy of Training

The rapid growth of counselling training at advanced level include the growth of jobs, the increasingly high profile of the work nationally, and finally the aspirations of practicing counsellors for professional status. I note in the latest (1996) BAC Training Directory the introduction of a 3 star category of training course, typically a masters degree for experienced practitioners, although most accredited courses are still 2 star. A useful way of looking at the kaleidoscope of training opportunities would be to see it as essentially a 3 tier hierarchy with introductory and intermediate as well as advanced levels. See Figure 1:-

Figure 1: A Training Hierarchy

Level (NVQ)	Qualn.	Ave. Taught Hours	Ave. Total Hours	Years Full or Part Time	Typical Entry Reqs.	Rationale
1 Intro. (2)	Foundation Course	20	80	0.5 pt	-	Curiosity Skill devel.
2 Interm. (3/4)	Certificate	100	300	1-2 pt	Fdn. Couns. Relevant emp. Vol. work	Career devel. Skill devel.
3 Advanced (4/5)	Diploma	450	1350	1 ft, 2-3 pt	Cert. Couns. Degree or equiv. Much experience	New career. BAC accredn.
	MA/MSc	600	1800	1-2 ft, 2-4 pt	Dip. Couns. Degree or equiv.	Senior posns. Academic career
	Phd	-	5,400	3 ft, 6+ pt	Degree/ Dip.	Top jobs

The current situation is very confusing for the budding trainee and there are as yet no universally agreed definitions of terms and standards. However, the systematic introduction of agreed national vocational qualifications (NVQs) and BAC accreditation are bringing some much needed clarity. In the meantime the above table should be viewed as very approximate. My own 1995 survey of advanced courses showed that most are aiming at BAC accreditation which will involve a minimum of 250 hours of theory and 200 of skill development plus some supervised practice. Teaching methods will include lectures, seminars, workshops and work placement. Assessment will involve some combination of essays, case studies, skills group and placement supervisor reports, personal diaries, and seen or unseen exams, but the trend is clearly away from exams towards continuous assessment. There will be an essential

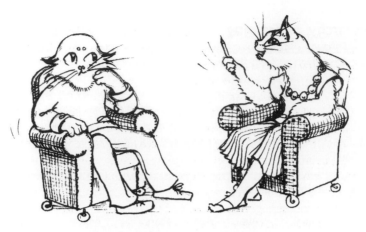

Before training . . . "if I were you"

element of personal development or therapy ranging from attendance at a regular group for the duration of the course to individual counselling/therapy for a specified minimum number of hours. Seeing real clients will be seen as the acid test and meetings with placement supervisor and/or academic tutor will normally involve taped conversations with selected clients. As a rough guide your total commitment will amount to a grand total of about three times the number of timetabled contact hours for the course.

A typical breakdown for a recognised advanced diploma course would be as follows:–

i	Lectures/seminars	250 hours
ii	Workshops	200 hours
iii	Personal development	50 hours
iv	Supervised practice	100 hours
v	Private study	750 hours
	Grand total	1350 hours

Costs and competition for places vary enormously but according to Careers Service Trust (1996) BAC accredited courses are becoming increasingly more sought after in spite of being much more expensive. See Figure 2:–

Figure 2: Cost and Competition (Advanced diplomas, 1996)

	Accredited Courses	Non-accredited
Average ratio of applicants to places	6.3	3.1
Increased competition for places (1994-6)	+ 46%	+ 11%
Average Fees	£3,650	£2,100

Public funding for counselling students is now very limited although some individuals might possibly be supported by their LEA (discretionary grant) and BAC offer a few bursaries. Some full time students are seconded on full salary by their employers as training is itself a growth industry, and employers may be willing to assist financially with part time counselling courses if this can be seen to benefit the organisation. Another reason why some people prefer part time to full time study is that it does not normally affect their entitlement to welfare benefits.

The vast majority of counselling students are self financed from their own savings or by borrowing from relatives, friends or the banks. The Department of Employment in conjunction with three banks (Barclays, Co-op and Clydesdale) offers Career Development Loans of £300 to £5,000, with repayments starting three months after finishing the course, but clearly there is an element of risk as there are no guarantees of counselling employment and initial earnings in private practice may be very modest. In my time I have come across some bizarre cases of funding including the MSc student (not in counselling) who, because of a spell of six months unemployed, was judged to be 'training' and therefore eligible for benefits (i.e. an income) and a weekly training allowance. Full time students are not supposed to receive welfare benefits because they are not 'available for employment'. In practice course leaders are usually familiar with how all their students are coping financially with their training and are unlikely to miss a trick.

Motives for Change and Development

Ben Ball (1996) in his excellent guide to personal and professional development, summarizes the most commonly cited reasons for dissatisfaction with people's current work situation.

i   Lack of opportunity for reward and growth in one's job.
ii   Lack of challenge or excitement.
iii   Lack of commitment to, and understanding of, the organisation's goals.
iv   Lack of information about oneself and the organisation.
v   Crisis management.

Ben Ball's work satisfaction rating is reproduced and summarised here with his permission. Please circle one of the numbers against each statement:

	Agree				Disagree
I feel relatively successful in what I do	5	4	3	2	1
On balance, my work is satisfying	5	4	3	2	1
I can use my skills to good effect	5	4	3	2	1
I have access to training and development	5	4	3	2	1
I feel positive about my career prospects	5	4	3	2	1
I don't feel valued at work	1	2	3	4	5
I'd like more reward from my work	1	2	3	4	5
There's little opportunity to discuss my career plans	1	2	3	4	5
I feel that I have outgrown my job	1	2	3	4	5
I often wish I could change direction	1	2	3	4	5

Scores over 40. You seem quite happy with your current lot, but this is not necessarily an excuse for inaction. You will still need to identify your development needs in order to maintain your level of motivation.

Between 20 and 40. Your satisfaction with work could obviously be improved. Are there particular issues which need your attention? Greater level of reward? Lack of challenge? Untapped skills? Identify the primary issues before drawing up an action plan.

20 and below. You may need to take some urgent steps to avoid stress or burnout. Either your line manager should be aware of your feelings through regular appraisal or, alternatively, you may need to find a mentor figure who can support you. Almost certainly you will benefit from professional careers counselling to explore your options for development and change.

Source: 'Assessing Your Career: Time for a Change?' by Ben Ball, BPS Books, 1996 pp. 90-2.

Range of Courses

Person centred (or client centred) and psychodynamic counselling respectively are the two models which are most widely taught and practiced in Britain but because of the widespread and growing acceptance of eclectic and integrated approaches you can reasonably expect advanced courses to introduce and discuss various models. Sometimes the emphasis on the person centred or psychodynamic approach is clear from the title and courses in cognitive, Gestalt and TA will be clearly labelled. Scrutiny of the detailed syllabus is advisable to ensure that you are emotionally, philosophically and intellectually in tune with the course. The following sample from the BAC Training Directory illustrates the range of advanced established courses:–

   i   **Training Course in Person Centred Therapy** (BAC accredited). Offered by PCT (Britain). 2 years 8 months part time, 6 residential weeks, 21 supervision days and individual supervision. No formal qualifications required, selection on written statement, personal reference and interview. On-going counselling experience essential.

   ii   **Diploma in Advanced Psychodynamic Counselling** (BAC accredited). Westminster Pastoral Foundation. 1 year full time and 1 year part time, or 3-4 years part time. Entry by casework experience, basic counselling skills training, self development work and appropriate life experience.

   iii   **Diploma in Counselling** (BAC accredited). University of Bristol. 2 years part time, 1 afternoon & evening per week + 1 weekend per term. Degree or equivalent, some training in counselling, work setting in which sustained practice possible.

   iv   **Diploma in Cognitive Approaches to Counselling and Psychotherapy.** Goldsmiths College, University of London. 2 years part time. Entry by professional qualification in social science or counselling or 2 years relevant professional experience.

   v   **Training in Gestalt** (accredited by the Gestalt Psychotherapy Training Institute). Manchester Gestalt Centre. 3 years minimum part time, for qualified professionals in caring roles.

vi **Training in Transactional Analysis** (accredited by International Transactional Analysis Association and European Association for TA). Iron Mill Centre. 4 years weekends. Professional qualification in a caring profession or degree in psychology or appropriate counselling qualification.

vii **Diploma in Integrative Psychosynthesis Counselling** (BAC accredited). Communication & Counselling Foundation. 3 years part time, 2 days per month. Entry by interview and 5 day foundation course.

After training

It is now possible to take a (funded) full time bachelor's degree in Psychology and Counselling at Roehampton Institute and 4 year part time degrees are available in Counselling and Mental Health (City University) and Therapeutic Counselling (Manchester Met. Univ.). However, counselling is not for the 18 year old school leaver and the 26 year old lower age limit for Manchester doesn't surprise me. Judicious choice of training and related experience can have a major impact on your career prospects. For example working as a lay worker with predominantly elderly people, together with voluntary work and training in substance abuse, will improve your chances of working in medical settings.

There are specialised training courses for those who want to work with particular clients and/or settings:–

i **Medical.** Mostly at introductory level, for dealing with clients and their families concerned with AIDS/HIV, substance abuse, cancer, complementary medicine, fertility, genetics, mental health, psychosexuality, terminal illness. Several courses are aimed generally at health care settings. The British Association for Psychotherapy, three universities (Bristol, Keele and Strathclyde), and three other colleges (City of Manchester, Gwent, and Ripon & York St. John) offer postgraduate diploma courses in counselling in primary health care. The potential employers of this expertise include district health authorities, NHS Trusts and general practices.

ii **Education.** A variety of institutions offer courses for counselling children or adolescents but problems of funding school counsellor posts have resulted in the demise of some diploma courses. The London Institute for Education do offer teachers a training in pastoral care and social education (not to be confused with 'pastoral care' in the religious sense) and the University of Nottingham has full time and part time courses in 'counselling studies' but, given the relatively healthy state of counselling in other educational settings I am surprised at the complete absence of advanced diplomas in student counselling. The potential employers include all public and private sector colleges and universities.

iii **Work.** The Universities of Bristol and Birmingham offer postgraduate diploma and certificate courses respectively in counselling at work, and a handful of FE colleges offer introductory courses. ICAS, CEPEC, and the Institute for Group Analysis offer courses for managers and supervisors. The potential employers are the those larger employers where trauma is commonplace (banks, building societies, uniformed and emergency services), those sophisticated enough to know how to get the very best out of their workforce and the providers of EAPs (Employee Assistance Programmes). There is considerable scope for private practice here.

iv **Pastoral Care.** The Westminster Pastoral Foundation are well established and validate a few courses around the country, and I understand that some non Christians choose their courses purely for the quality of their training. Other established organisations offering advanced training include the Clinical Theology Association, St George's Hospital, Bethlem Royal and Maudsley Special Health Authority, and Birmingham University Department of Theology. Youth With A Mission, based in London's east end, offer a 2 year diploma in Christian counselling. Potential employers include religious organisations and charities.

v **Community.** Training courses, mostly at introductory level, are available for counselling particular client groups including men, women, young people, bereaved people, perpetrators/victims of sexual abuse, substance misuse, and ethnic minorities. Many courses (up to MSc level) are aimed at couples or families and of course working with groups is a major specialism in its own right. Leading organisations offering training in this area include the Institute of Family Therapy, London Marriage Guidance, the Tavistock Institute of Marital Studies, and the Universities of Kent and Leicester. Potential employers include local authorities and charities, and relationship concerns feature strongly in private practice.

The market in counselling training is quite volatile with new courses springing up and others falling by the wayside. Growth has taken place mostly by new courses rather than existing courses expanding, with an average of around 25 students in each intake. But some courses are struggling on with small numbers and there is no way that the 25% annual growth rate of counselling training places in the early 1990s can be sustained. The overall growth of counselling jobs will be less spectacular, with the average number of applicants already 20 for each advertised job and rising, and potential students will hopefully be aware of this. The south east in general and London in particular offer the widest range of counselling training and elsewhere in Britain choice may be quite limited. However, some courses are run as a series of modules often at weekends and may be residential for those willing to travel out of their area. Modular courses, which are made up of sets of discrete, individually assessed units, are sweeping the country at all levels (now even A-level). Although the essence of counselling training is the integration of theory, practice and personal development, it is still possible to exploit the advantages of modular structures such as flexibility and choice. Validating bodies such as BAC, examination boards and universities simply have to satisfy themselves which particular sets of modules meet their requirements.

There have been great advances in 'distance learning' following the success of the Open University and there are a number of Open Learning Courses now available which contain written and audio material. The Institute of Counselling offers programmes of residential schools throughout the year together with training in counselling skills at intermediate and advanced levels. Their more advanced courses have recognition by the Association of Christian Counsellors, and their research interests include post traumatic stress disorder and counselling disaster survivors and their families. The National Extension College have pioneered flexible forms of learning for adults and their courses include counselling skills, bereavement and loss, and setting up your own private practice. The OU Health and Social Welfare Courses do not provide professional training in counselling but do offer the opportunity to acquire related knowledge, expertise and qualifications. The OU is open to all, regardless of educational background, and flexible home study arrangements fit with students' work and lifestyle. The CATs points awarded may be transferred when relevant to degree and diploma programmes at other institutions.

The BAC Training Directory and POSTGRAD (the directory of graduate studies), which should be available in your local careers libraries, are the most reliable source of information on counselling courses, but in a rapidly changing scene you should check direct with your nearest universities and colleges of further and higher education. A word of caution: institutions of education are under pressures to register and hold on to increasing numbers of students and this can lead to prospectuses which frankly overstate the job prospects. Some course leaders will have information about jobs obtained by their graduates and they might even be willing to put you in touch with their alumni who have agreed to act as helpful contacts. This is common practice in universities that have large and well resourced careers centres.

NVQs, SQVs and CATs

The National Council for Vocational Qualifications (NCVQ, and SQVs for Scotland) oversees the development of qualifications linked to occupational standards. The development of S/NVQs has been a very significant move to provide an alternative to academic qualifications, especially A-levels which are equivalent to S/NVQ level 3. A degree is equivalent to level 4 and post-graduate study level 5. Financial support from the Department of Employment enabled representatives of industry to determine standards of competence in their vocational area. These representatives formed groups called Lead Bodies and by 1994 The 'Advice, Guidance, Counselling and Psychotherapy Lead Body' (AGC&PLB) was formed. Qualification frameworks, which comprise explicit units which make up occupational standards, have now been agreed for the following qualifications:–

Level 2 Service Support (aimed at people who have the first contact with clients).
Level 3 Advice (aimed at, for example, Citizens Advice and Welfare Rights)

Level 4 Advice (aimed at specialist practitioners with a substantial degree of autonomy)

Level 3 Guidance (aimed at, for example, those working in careers or educational or adult guidance, who are supervised by a line manager)

Level 4 Guidance (aimed at, for example, careers officers and adult guidance advisors who manage their own casework).

The AGC&PLB has selected its initial Awarding Bodies and they are City and Guilds, EDEXCEL, BTEC, the Local Government Management Board, the Institute of Careers Guidance, the Open University Validation Service, RSA, and SCOTVEC. These organisations, or your employer, can advise you how your accredited prior learning (APL) can help towards these qualifications. These previous disparate bodies will thus be brought under the same umbrella and the levels of qualifications will be more clear.

In their March Information sheet 1997 Sue Slipman, Chair of AGC&PLB, was pleased to announce that they have been invited to bid to become one of the new training organisations (NTOs) that will replace the existing network of lead bodies. The name will change to CAMPAG which is an anagram of the sectors of Counselling, Advice, Mediation, Psychotherapy, Advocacy and Guidance. The timetable for publication of AGC&PLB Standards was:-

No. Evidence Routes	To be Published	
3	Summer 1997	Mediation (anticipated level 4)
up to 5	Autumn 1997	Generic Counselling (ant. level 3)
up to 5	Autumn 1997	Couples Counselling (ant. level 4 or 5)
up to 5	"	Therapeutic Counselling (ant. level 4 or 5)
up to 8	"	Psychotherapy (ant. level 4 or 5)

(Information point 01438 840511).

The accreditation processes of BAC and British Psychological Society (BPS) are likely to be adapted eventually to match those qualifications approved by the S/NCVQ. BAC guidelines already make strong recommendations for GPs to employ only those counsellors who have accreditation in terms of both training and practice, and local guidelines via Family Health Services Authorities are in place in many areas.

British higher education awards are increasingly seen in terms of credit accumulation. For example, an honours degree is regarded as 360 CAT (Credit Accumulation and Transfer) credits, with 120 points each at levels I, II and III. A full time student will normally earn the award by accumulating all the required credits in three successive years of study. But many wishing to study for a degree have already achieved learning which may be measured and converted to CAT credits. Such learning is often reflected by the possession of formal qualifications, but may also be claimed

Many years later

for experience via written evidence and interview. Voluntary counselling, when properly supervised, may well qualify in this respect.

My interpretation of all this is that paper qualifications will increasingly become explicit, modular (or unitary) in structure, and will increasingly count.

Typical Student Profile

In spring 1995 I conducted a sample survey of 100 students on advanced counselling courses (3 BAC recognised and 3 other) and came to the following conclusions:–

i   Average age 43, 70% female.
ii   89% have degrees and/or professional qualifications.
iii   For 63% the motivation to train is current paid or voluntary work.
iv   For 65% counselling is a significant element of current paid work.
v   76% are engaged in voluntary work in mostly community and medical settings.
vi   In the short term (next 5 years) aspirations include:–
    *   50% to work in part time paid counselling and 20% full time.
    *   Most preferred settings are private practice (48%), medical (27%) and community 23%).
    *   70% view prospects for counselling in their preferred settings as good or very good.
    *   54% are fairly confident and 43% even more confident of achieving their short term goals.
    *   57% identify financial constraints, including 23% giving up their current job.
vii   Long term aspirations are equal between part time and full time paid counselling.

However, according to my own survey of 20 advanced counselling course leaders only two settings, medical (14 mentions) and work related (10 mentions), are thought likely to experience significant growth in counselling jobs. My own information and experience suggests that further and higher education will also enjoy some growth in counselling and related guidance work. Counselling trainees may well be underestimating the difficulties of setting up and succeeding in private practice. Attitudes towards counselling as a career are varied with some students content to engage in expensive and rigorous training in order to enhance their current jobs or voluntary work. Male students tend to be more confident than females about achieving their counselling career aims but this is not explained by relative ability. As I have argued elsewhere (Ross 1993), men in this age range may be more single minded about careers whereas the women aim for more balanced lives. There is most certainly no single stereotype counsellor and regardless of your theoretical preferences, age, gender, ethnic group, disability or sexual orientation there are opportunities out there for you.

Case Study

Susan is 36 years old with 2 children of school age and an architect husband. At the age of 20 she dropped out of polytechnic after one year because of an unplanned pregnancy and never got around to resuming her studies. Her second child developed leukemia and she derived much support from a self help she started up with another parent. She is a natural listener, able to resist the temptation to give advice, and is regularly sought out by family, friends and even work colleagues who like to confide in her. She works as a part time careers information assistant/receptionist at the local university and particularly enjoys the client contact. After her mother died suddenly she trained as a voluntary bereavement counsellor and later enrolled on the certificate course offered by the local university department of external studies. She has been much encouraged by the feedback from course tutors and others who have indicated that she has all the right qualities for a career in guidance or counselling. The minister at her local methodist church has suggested she apply for the part time post of lay worker which is coming up (not advertised) and she received further inspiration from attending a lecture on counselling the victims of torture. Her husband fully supports her desire to develop a career in counselling. What should she do next?

The options are wide with the most promising settings in which to work being medical, education and pastoral care. Her employers have offered to pay for the certificate course in careers guidance in higher education, which might be a springboard for eventually working as a student counsellor, but are not prepared to finance certificate or diploma courses in counselling. She eventually decided to work in primary health care and started with just 5 hours per week in a nearby large general practice whilst still studying for the diploma in counselling (BAC accreditation expected). Being very good at the work and being highly regarded by both her placement supervisor and therapist (diploma course), the opportunity arose to set up in private practice, initially working from home. There were no shortage of referrals from these sources and there was never any need to advertise. By choice she continues to work in general practice and limits herself to 10 private clients per week that she charges on a sliding scale. Because of her growing reputation she has been approached by a large employer to do some redundancy counselling following a management reorganisation, and she is considering an invitation to assist in the training of volunteer bereavement counsellors.

Conclusions

The majority of counselling advertised vacancies already ask for BAC accreditation or equivalent and for 'equivalent' read training courses of similar length and quality to those already recognised. There is a complex and crowded training marketplace out there in which some advanced courses that are struggling to keep up their student numbers and/or are unlikely to obtain accreditation are going to fall by the wayside. One good way to decide on your training priorities is to identify the most desirable potential employers in your locality and work backwards. Ask for their views on the value of particular training courses and also they might be able to put you in touch with recent graduates of those courses. In large organisations the personnel managers are the experts on recruitment and training, and if they are not themselves familiar with the details of preferred counselling qualifications then they will know who is. They will know where exactly the power resides when it comes to making counsellor appointments.

Those who insist on the intrinsic superiority of single theoretical approaches (and any given one in particular) are a declining minority and longer term relative job security is more likely with broadly based training and experience. Universities and colleges of further education are heavily involved in counselling training but some independent institutes continue to thrive, especially those enjoying BAC accreditation. The former will tend to follow the rhythms of the academic year, with part time courses offered on half days or evenings during term time, whereas the latter are more likely to offer intensive training at weekends. If your early experiences of counselling training are very positive then you could be thinking in terms of investment in the region of £3,000 to £5,000 to make counselling into a second or third career and if you can persuade your current employer to help with those costs then you will be fortunate indeed. The judgement you will exercise on training options will itself be based on a heady brew of intellect, intuition and faith.

A heady brew of intellect, intuition and faith

CHAPTER 3:
COUNSELLING IN MEDICAL SETTINGS

Introduction

Hospitals, general practices and mental health related community projects represent exciting, challenging and sometimes chaotic settings for working as a counsellor and the CMS is the fastest growing division of the BAC. There will be increased opportunities not only for nurses and other paramedics to specialise in counselling, but also for others with non medical backgrounds. The coverage in most areas of the UK is patchy but it does seem as though counselling is well on its way to recognition in primary health care and, to a lesser extent, in secondary care. Treatments such as acupuncture have become increasingly popular in recent years and it is not unusual for counselling, a 'talking cure', to be available alongside these in 'Alternative Health' Centres. In practice the debate often centres on drugs versus counselling, with doctors amongst the first to admit that medication or other drastic forms of intervention are frequently inappropriate.

The Community Care Act of 1990 and reforms designed to promote a complete family health service gave a major boost for counselling in primary care, and now fund-holding general practices have increased flexibility to purchase complementary treatments such as acupuncture and counselling, or to employ such staff directly. The DoH (1993) clearly identified the need for counselling and psychotherapy. These guidelines include the detection of at-risk groups and the provision of advice and counselling, for example in connection with unemployment, genetic risks, misuse of drugs, and stress management. It suggests joint working arrangements with voluntary and statutory organisations which sounds to me like the green light for counselling in medical and community settings to develop in partnership. However, value for money will have to be demonstrated and then the demand for counsellors to be registered with a professional body, and to have completed a recognised training, will surely follow.

Medical and Interpersonal Models

American counselling practice has shifted adherence from a medical, symptoms oriented model of treatment towards an interpersonal, holistic one. An interpersonal model has enabled nurses to develop and integrate their skills of listening and responding to patients' needs, skills which would become increasingly identified as counselling skills. Project 2000, one of the most modern and progressive forms of nurse training, now includes counselling in the curriculum. Many people visit their doctors for medical solutions to non-medical problems; hence the need for counselling services as part of a supportive framework that includes appropriate treatment, health promotion clinics and self-help groups.

The situation in secondary health care is similar to that of primary care 10 to 15 years ago and counselling is gradually emerging as a distinct form of treatment. Many counsellors' main role will be nursing or occupational therapy etc and doctors may have been more familiar with the practices of clinical psychology or psychotherapy than with counselling as a discipline in its own right. By comparison the hospice movement has attracted a great deal of public support and counselling has been combined with expert palliative medicine in order to meet the needs of terminally ill patients and their families. East (1995) likens counselling in primary care and secondary care to teaching, with the former being the generalist and the latter being the specialist. In secondary care counsellors tend to define or specify their role as being linked to a primary occupational identity together with additional information about the particular disease, medical condition or areas of work in which they specialize, for example HIV/AIDS or post-traumatic stress.

According to Mann (1993) 10 to 15% of the population have mental health problems at any one time, with the most common presenting concerns being anxiety and depression. Strathdee and Sutherby (1993) conclude that up to a quarter of all consultations to an average GP's daily surgeries have a significant mental health component and a substantial saving in the drugs budget is possible when alternative provision such as counselling is available. Ten times the number of people with all kinds of psychiatric disorder attend primary care services than are referred to psychiatrists (Goldberg and Huxley 1993) and counselling is generally regarded as less stigmatizing than psychiatric referral. The health of individuals may be affected by their family systems as Skinner and Cleese (1983) have shown to a wide audience. If specific diseases are in fact the result of complex interaction of biopsychosocial factors, then counselling and psychotherapy in medical settings would be regarded not as a replacement for medical treatment but as necessary and complementary to the healing process.

Effectiveness and Constraints

The radical health care reforms following the new GP contract (1990) have accelerated the growth of counselling in primary health care. According to East (1995) the scheme in Derbyshire models the principles of good practice with strict criteria of training, experience and supervision. The pattern nationally could be one of initial resistance followed by incorporation, an increase in training and new qualifications with the medical network extending to include the new specialism. Counselling provision can be idiosyncratic in nature but, encouragingly, over 30% of general practices have counsellors and 80% of GPs without a counsellor wish to provide one. Understandably the counsellor's work reflects the doctor's perception of their competence, with psychiatric nurses seen to be ideal for management of psychiatric illness and clinical psychologists suitable for obsessions and phobias. Bereaved patients would ideally see a practice counsellor.

Although evidence is so far limited East (1995) is optimistic about research findings and very positive conclusions were also reached by Monach and Monro (1993) in Sheffield and Harrison (1993) in Oxfordshire. Thomas and Corney (1993) found high levels of satisfaction among GPs for counselling and community practice services and my own survey of BAC members showed that GPs were one of three major sources of referral of clients to private practitioners. According to MIND (1993) people consistently demonstrate that they value being able to choose alternatives to medication, but 'talking treatments' are limited nationally, especially for some groups

"clinical psychologist for phobias"

such as ethnic minorities, the less well off, or homosexuals who have little or no access to them.

MIND (1993) offer the Marylebone Health Centre as a model of good practice in the NHS. The impressive range of treatments include traditional and complementary medicine, stress classes, counselling, referrals to long-term psychotherapy, and healing services are held once a month at the Marylebone Church next door. Befriending, practical advice and help is also available for welfare issues such as housing, and the Centre operates telephone helplines staffed by volunteers who are vetted, trained and supervised by the staff of the Community Outreach Unit. The budget for psychotropic drugs has been dramatically reduced to one-third of the £80,000 typically spent by the average GP in a year.

Tyndall (1993) points out that doctors, nurses and similar professionals, with their ingrained patterns of caring that involves action and problem-solving, might find it difficult to adopt the outwardly more passive stance of counselling. Learning how be a creative and effective expert and yet not give advice can be a slow process! East (1995) states that medical settings show a scene of occupational rivalry set against a background of hierarchical structures, archaic assumptions and vocational stereotyping:–

"Doctors are clever, well-educated and therefore entitled to lead others; nurses are academically limited and therefore entitled to serve others. Neither or these historical stereotypes do justice to reality but are still played out . . . the rules of engagement are clear to all, even if they are never articulated." (East 1995: 110)

However, the overall picture is very encouraging, with counsellors becoming valued members of the health care team. Following the successful launch of guidelines for general practice (BAC 1993b) attention in the division has switched to the needs of counsellors in hospital settings.

Because they mostly work alone with their clients, one of the most widely expressed concerns of counsellors is their sense of isolation, despite apparently surrounded by other caring professionals. But as Aveline (1992: p128) has pointed out:–

"to disclose personal problems was to invite the accusation of undesirable weakness from others, and from their internalised role model which stated that carers have to be strong."

"the rules of engagement are clear"

The question 'who cares for the carers?', such as nurses and counsellors, is often asked but rarely answered satisfactorily and the costs of inadequate support can be enormous in terms of staff turnover, sickness and absenteeism. House (in Dryden, 1995) identifies many sources of stress working in general practices including 'frame insecurity', very damaged clients (so-called 'heartsink' or 'fat envelope' patients), clashes over drug prescribing, flawed referral process, and junior/unprofessionalised status. In the same book Bond analyses the stresses of working with clients with HIV/AIDS, such as confidentiality management and (irrational) fears of infection.

Maybe counselling should be a part-time career and that would suit many people, especially women. One counsellor who works primarily with nurses is Kirsten:-

A Day in the Life of Kirsten (early 40s)
Susan. Last night a patient on Susan's ward died a peaceful and dignified death, which brought into sharp focus the fact that, after two years, our own work together was coming to an end. In almost classic textbook style Susan became very tearful and shaky and wondered whether she was ready to end counselling. I acknowledged her fears, some 'old' material was discussed again, and our termination date remained unchanged. I have learned a lot from Susan and I felt some sadness too.

Jutta. 6 weeks ago Jutta's mother died in a plane crash and she felt depressed, suicidal and very guilty that she had seen so little of her mother. She appears to have worked through many issues including intense anger and emotional pain caused when her mother left her father. She has been looking at photographs and talking to her sister and this has helped her a lot. This short period of intense work felt unusually complete and I almost felt like celebrating, a rare response for me.

Terry. Terry telephoned to say that both his union rep. and his manager had suggested that he talk to me. I clarify, as usual, that he himself really wants to see me and then he breaks down and explains that he has been suspended from duty. My heart sinks with this kind of call because I am usually presented with a nurse who is totally devastated, but fortunately I can at least make an appointment for Terry tomorrow. Sitting alongside staff as they go through this very painful episode in their career does make me feel sad. In such a pressurized world we are all capable of making mistakes or errors of judgement and I admire clients' willingness to work hard with me on this.

Other parts of the day were taken up with administration, meetings, phone-calls, and a session with a supervisee. Re-arranging an appointment reminds me of the need to be flexible when you counsel in medical settings. After a tearful call from a staff nurse I finish work at 6.30 pm. Time for a quick supper and then I'm off to the theatre.

Jobs, Supervision and Training
I analysed 175 jobs in medical settings advertised in the British Association for Counselling Jobfile over a four month period in 1995/6, all of which explicitly required a counselling qualification or counselling skills. There was a similar number of jobs which involved caring and/or supportive work, for which counselling experience would be advantageous. Most of these jobs were full-time and sometimes required professional qualifications such as occupational therapy, nursing or social work .

i   General (40) sometimes related to particular client groups and mostly in a hospital setting.

ii   Substance abuse (39), mostly in community or hospital settings.

iii   HIV/AIDS (24), usually in an NHS setting.

iv   Breast care (10).

v   Terminally ill (6)

vii   General Practice; Sexual Health (both 5).

viii   Occupational Health, usually for nurses in workplace; Cancer (4).

ix   Pain Relief; Disability (3).

x   Diabetes; Gynecology; Genetics; Vision Impairment; Eating Disorder; Family Planning (2).

xi   Respiratory Disease; Liver Transplant; Endocrinology; Blood Transfusion; Deafness; Parkinsons Disease; Gastro-enterology; Family Therapy; Rheumatology; Self Harm; Medical Staff; Victims of Medical Accidents; Returners from War Zones. (all one mention)

This illustrates the wide variety of counselling jobs related to medicine and there will be many more jobs in general practice although these will normally be advertised locally, if at all, and are much more likely to be part-time for around £15 per hour. Health care counsellors are employed on an extremely wide variety of contracts and pay scales, with a salary range from around £10,000 to £23,000 with the median £17,000. In general practice some work an agreed number of hours for nothing on the understanding that the GPs will refer some clients to be seen privately.

Supervision is all about monitoring, developing and supporting counsellors, is an important element of the BAC Code of Practice, and is also about maintaining standards. Ongoing supervision (a requirement for BAC accreditation) enables counsellors, especially those working alone, to obtain expert support and help from their most experienced peers, often in a group. Other professions with less strong traditions of supervision may have difficulty in accepting the importance of supervision and employers are sometimes at best ambivalent, for example by being reluctant to pay for it. I have never questioned its value, especially when dealing with suicidal clients.

Obtaining the right experience and training is a recurring theme of this book and there will be many opportunities for voluntary or modestly paid work in your locality that will help to launch or develop a counselling career in medical settings. For example, drop-in centres for ex-psychiatric patients or substance abusers are often short of volunteers and if you do not feel ready for counselling itself then you can make a start by making the tea or driving the minibus. Samaritons gain valuable experience with the people who may harm themselves, and there are many self help and support groups for the sufferers of cancer, schizophrenia etc and their families. Why not decide today to make a contribution? Your local social services department, hospital or general practice will have details of opportunities. Where a group is needed why not start one up?

Never underestimate the value and relevance of your own unique experience. Apart from a brief placement in a university health centre I have never worked as a counsellor in medical settings, but as I wrack my brains I recall that I have stage managed a 'section 25', dealt with depression, talked a client out of consuming a lethal cocktail of drugs and alcohol, accompanied patients to their assessment by a psychiatrist (and been asked my opinion), run relaxation classes for exam anxious students, quit smoking groups, counselled students of varied ages trying to cope with ME, glandular fever, insomnia, life threatening disease, high anxiety, drink problems, drug problems, anorexia etc etc. I have personally survived clinical depression and cancer. I might get in touch with my own GP and offer to help run a 'well man' clinic!

The increased professionalism and recognition of counselling in medical settings is demonstrated by the introduction of new Diplomas in Counselling in Primary Health Care sponsored by the Counselling in Primary Care Trust. Applicants should have BAC or equivalent and supervised experience and there is the possibility of a bursary from the Trust. There is also a one-year Counselling in Primary Health Care course offered by the British Association of Psychotherapists (BAP). There are many courses (source 1996 BAC Training Directory) related to medical settings, of which some are aimed at staff, such as ENB A10 Course in Counselling Theory and Practice, and others are related to specific problems such as Basic AIDS Counselling and the Diploma in Alcohol Counselling and Consultation. Special training in recognizing psychiatric illness and the effects of prescribed drugs will be essential for counsellors with non medical backgrounds. One university validated advanced 'training course' I know of is in effect an unpaid job of 'associate counsellor' in an NHS setting. In exchange for an agreed number of supervised hours with clients most of the fees are paid, thus bringing down the real costs of qualifying to well below £1,000.

A Day in the Life of Mandy (early 30s)

Cancer Patient Liaison Nurse. I work for hospital units in a recently created post in London, coordinating the care of patients from ENT, Plastic Surgery, Radiotherapy, Oncology and Oral Surgery.

My day started on a positive note: a joint visit with a district nurse to **Gerry's** house had gone well. My immediate impression at our first meeting on the ward is that Gerry is a bit of a one for the ladies. He was about to undergo liver surgery and the ward nurses were concerned about his rehabilitation after surgery and how he was going to cope at home. The district nurse's work was was cut out for her because Gerry needed repeated explanation of the surgery and how he would learn to recover. Gerry was to undergo radiotherapy as an outpatient and would need long term follow up to his progress. I explained that I had passed his details on to the radiotherapy specialist nurse who would also be meeting with the dietician.

My next stop was the radiotherapy department to see **Brian**, my very first referral in this new job. Brian, a 46 year old married man, had left a cancer growing on his hand that he had first noticed 15 years ago. He had cared for the growing wound himself and concealed his disfigurement, even from his wife, with washable bandages until he could stave off the inevitable no longer. He was taken to casualty with complications. Brian agreed to radiotherapy treatment to try to save his hand. "Cor, my wife's giving me grief. She's angry with me" he said as I closed the door to the rest of the world. I tentatively suggested that she might also be angry with herself (she has readily accepted my offer of a referral for counselling herself). He kept repeating how sorry he was "but that's the way I am". It was important to Brian that as few people as possible knew the extent of his disfigurement. Together we planned the 'dressing team': I would see him next week to visit his GP practice to provide both a resource as well as a support.

At lunchtime I grab a sandwich and meet up with **Roberta**, a 47 year old teacher, who has requested a meeting with the MacMillan nurse for her area at the local hospice. She knows there is still the possibility of drastic surgery but I get the impression that she will not accept it because, at best, the chances of both survival and reasonable quality of life are poor. She has already had a 2 month spell in hospital undergoing 4 operations and does not fancy another visit. She has a remarkably resilient sense of humour and spent most of her time in hospital writing a comedy for her local drama society. She gives me a ticket for tonight's performance and I have to make a hasty arrangement for a babysitter as my husband won't be home until late. Roberta is much reassured by the discussion of how symptoms and pain can be effectively controlled whether she remains at home or comes into the hospice. She is especially pleased to discover that MacMillan nurses work with survivors as well as so-called terminally ill patients. She is also going to get in touch with the Bristol Cancer Help Clinic. She is a fighter and has the advantage of a very supportive and loving husband.

My next stop was the renal unit who had telephoned the previous day asking if I could advise on **Bill's** care. Bill is a very vulnerable man in what felt like desperate circumstances. He was about to go through a divorce, was about to be homeless and said he had no one in whom he could confide, with the possible exception of a few drinking mates. When I saw him in clinic he was offered radical surgery and had the added complication of renal failure. He had been helped in his decision to undergo surgery, and a referral to a social worker enabled an application for housing to be urgently processed. While his dressings were being done he talked about nothing in particular and this was OK as he began to relax. I have now missed someone in another clinic and I make a mental note to follow that one up.

As I arrive back in the office I received a call to see **Mabel** who was having trouble with her feeding tube. Mabel is 81 years old and it was lovely to see her, with her bright shining eyes. The tube was put right and Mabel chatted for a while. Her daughter shed a few tears.

I just made it to the fortnightly meeting with a clinical nurse specialist in psychological medicine: an hour of tea and discussion about patients and issues is helpful to me. I am privy to his new book proposal which is a good reminder that there is another world out there from the world of cancer. Always my last job of the day, my telephone messages. I have seven and the last one was to let me know that a new tube I had shown and fitted to a patient with a long-term tracheostomy was, in her words, wonderful and so much more comfortable. Great! After giving my son Sean his tea and settling him down for the night I am off to the village hall to see Roberta's play.

Typical Jobs:–

1 Counsellor in Primary Care

Job Title:	Counsellor in Primary Care
Place of Work:	Group Practice, London
Employed by:	Dr. Smith and Partners
Responsible to:	Practice Development and Fundholding Manager
Salary:	£15 per hour
Contract:	One year with an option to renew until March 1997
Hours of Work:	Up to 80 per month
Holiday Entitlement:	5 weeks per annum plus one week study leave

Main Purpose of Job

To provide a counselling service to patients registered with the practice. Patients will be referred either as individuals or with others and an average of 6 sessions may be offered.

Person Specification

Education and Professional Qualifications

Essential: 450 hours of initial counselling training (BAC approved or equivalent).

Desirable: Full BAC accreditation or equivalent (UKCP)

Knowledge
Desirable: A knowledge of psychotropic drugs and their side effects. An understanding of at least two theoretical approaches to counselling.

Skills
Essential: Communication with clients and other professionals. Work with individuals.
Develop a rapport and maintain counselling relationships.
Desirable: Work with couples, families and groups.

Experience
Desirable: At least 350 hours of supervised counselling over at least 2 years.

Supervision
Essential: Currently in counselling supervision. Recognition of own strengths and weaknesses and the ability to identify own training needs.

Personal Attributes
Essential: Work with a broad range of clients, work as a member of a team, reliability and dependability, manage personal conflict and be aware of own value and limits, accept and adopt change, a flexible approach and monitor own stress levels and to be capable of working under pressure.

Equal Opportunities
Essential: Awareness and understanding of equal opportunity issues.

Pay and Conditions
Funding is secured until March 1997. The pay includes an allowance for personal supervision fees and professional insurance There is no pension scheme.

Application Form
Personal Details: Education (school and college) and qualifications; Employment (position, duties, reasons for leaving); References (2); and, most important,
"Tell about any experience, knowledge or skills you have which are relevant to the job" (including unpaid work or activities outside work).

2 Counsellor in Secondary Health Care

Position:	Counsellor (part-time) Oncology Unit
Grade:	6
Salary	£14,779 -£17,291 pro-rata
Hours	12 per week
Qualifications:	Recognized qualification in Counselling.
	BAC Accreditation (or working towards this)
Accountable to:	Dr. Jones, Consultant, Oncology Unit
	Dr. Williams, Manager, Cancer Services
Annual leave	20 days per year (rising to 25 after 10 years)
Superannuation:	Employers pay two thirds of contributions. Pension scheme.

Job Summary
Responsibility for the counselling of in-patients and out-patients referred by the Oncology team.
Facilitation of support groups for patients, or staff, if required.

Person Specification

Essential	Desirable
Recognised qualifications in counselling .	BAC Accreditation or working towards this. Previous experience working in a health care setting.
Experience in working as independent practitioner.	IT experience/skills.
Some knowledge of Health Service requirements	Recognised teaching skills and/or evidence of management of informal and formal teaching sessions.
Knowledge of audit process. Previous teaching experience. Professional updating.	Previous function in working as a team member. Previous experience in support groups.

Application Form

Personal Details; References (2); Education and Qualifications; Employment History; Health Record (days off sick).

Supporting Information (Please tell us why you have applied for this post and give a brief summary of your relevant experience and skills).

3 Drug and HIV Support Worker in an Independent Charity

Main Functions

i Provide an assessment and counselling service to the Clinic's clients, ensuring that they are properly assessed for treatment and that their social care problems are appropriately addressed.

ii Provide pre and post test counselling for patients seeking an HIV antibody test and to provide a supportive range of services including safer drug use and safer sex.

Person Specification

Essential Qualifications: CQSW, Dip. SW, RMN/RGN or any other relevant qualification.

Training in HIV infection issues and counselling from an appropriate source e.g.. ENB 934 or any other recognised voluntary sector training.

Essential Experience	i Direct work with drug users.
	ii Experience in person centred counselling and group work.
	iii Advocacy and report writing .
Desirable Experience	i Experience of working with young people.
	ii Experience of working with the range of drug treatment and rehabilitation agencies, particularly residential rehabilitation programmes.
Knowledge	i Of drug use and HIV/AIDS issues, including illicit drug use and treatment programmes – essential.
	ii Of the welfare system – desirable.

Personal Qualities
Client empathy, self confidence, adaptability, patience, self motivation, and the ability to work as a team member.
Application Form
Personal Details; References; Present and Previous Employment; Education and Training.
Personal Statement (Please use the space below to tell us what qualities, experience and skills you can bring to the post. Give details of any professional, voluntary or other work and training that may have some bearing on your application).

Case Studies
I A Newcomer to General Practice:– Jane

Education

1995	University	Diploma in Counselling (incl. 40 hrs. of personal therapy)
1994		Certificate in Counselling
1979	College of FE	Teaching Certificate (FE)
1975		Certificate in Reality Therapy
1971	College of FE	Diploma in Careers Guidance
1970	Polytechnic	BA in Humanities

Work Experience

1994	University	Counsellor 4 hours per week (placement)
1989	University	Careers Counsellor, part-time (8 hours per week)
1980-85	Training Organisation	Tutor
1979-88	FE College	Part-time Lecturer and Tutor
1977-79	Careers Service	Careers Advisor
1974-76	School Commission Canada	School Counsellor: Personal and Careers Awarded membership of Association of Counsellors
1971-73	Careers Service	Student Guidance.

Other relevant experience includes school governor, teacher recruitment, conference speaker.
The Job
General Practice, 4 doctors: 6 hours per week at £15 per hour. Additional time for research and administration 3 hours unpaid. Supervision – 1 hour per month (paid by me).
Selection Procedure
35 minute panel interview (2 GPs and Practice Manager). I telephoned after the closing date and sent in my CV.
Household Context
Married, 2 teenage children.
Lucky Breaks
My first lucky break was getting the job of school counsellor in Canada, and the

second was the timing of this job. It came right at the end of my counselling course when my interest was flagging and the dissertation was getting bogged down. I had an incentive to complete both course and dissertation which is what I did.

Satisfactions

I meet the full range of age and class of people. I love working in partnership with caring doctors and appreciate the vast range of clients, e.g. a compulsive liar with troubled relationships, a woman raped 10 years ago, a patient with long-term severe depression.

Disappointments

Doctors' referrals can sometimes be erratic and sometimes it is not appropriate to stop seeing a client after just six sessions: for example I have continued to see a very depressed client for two years without charge. The rate of pay seems reasonable but not after all expenses are taken into account, such as supervision.

Surprises

The number of patients on anti-depressants.

The Future

I would like to do more GP work or train as a divorce mediator. They work in partnership with solicitors which saves on clients' legal fees in spite of the work being well paid at £60 per hour. Perhaps develop a specialism in group work or in brief counselling.

Advice To Budding Practice Counsellors

Be creative, distribute information about yourself, offer to work unpaid. You need flexibility of approaches to match wide range of clients.

Comment

Jane's first lucky break was the most important one as it created a snowball effect for working in Canada and later in the UK. She persuaded the Canadian embassy to permit her to work rather than be the dependant of a worker. Luck is where preparation meets opportunity and Jane is someone who tends to make her own.

Case Study of a Very Experienced Counsellor – Sheena (forties)

Work Experience

10 Years as a Social Worker and 6 Years as a Counsellor in a General Practice.

The Job

Senior Counsellor in an NHS Mental Health Counselling Centre: half time (18.5 hours) at £21,923 pa. There are the equivalent of four professional staff plus unpaid associates. All clients are all self referred. I also work in private practice.

Selection Procedure

Application form plus CV: shortlisted candidates met with the full team of staff and associates who gave feedback to the selection panel: final panel (6 person) interview.

Counselling Training

Registered UKCP Psychotherapist and BAC accredited Counsellor.

    i   Degree in Psychology
    ii   Postgrad. Diploma in Social Work

iii   In service training in social work over 10 years
iv   Training in counselling couples (Relate)
v   1 year training in group work (Institute of Group Analysis), costing £200
vi   Diploma in Humanistic Psychology
vii   1 year training in Gestalt Psychotherapy
viii   Diploma in Humanistic and Integrative Psychotherapy
ix   Variety of experiences as psychotherapy client (various orientations) culminating in 6 years in psychoanalytic psychotherapy (total cost around £8,000, tax deductible for private practice)

Household Context
Married with 3 teenage children: early child-care shared equally with both working part time

Satisfactions
Finding that people's capacity to really use the counselling relationship is not at all related to conventional intelligence or education (as per the literature) but the joint ability of counsellor and client to find a common language. Always absorbing and awe inspiring, never boring!

Disappointments
It is important to be able to accept the sometimes very limited nature of what you can can offer in the face of extremely distressed/damaged people in dire circumstances.

Surprises
When appreciation does come it is a pleasant surprise, not a need being satisfied. To discover people's amazing capacity for recovery/growth given the necessary conditions.

Lucky Breaks
Talking myself into a job of developing counselling training (youth) while acting as tutor visiting social work student on placement. Being welcomed by a GP with tremendous warmth and enthusiasm into the first job of counselling in general practice.

The Future
Unsure: I would like to be involved in developing further training for counselling in general practice. I would like to have more time for my own personal expression and freedom (painting, etc) alongside working with clients and providing supervision as I do now.

Advice (for budding NHS Counsellors)
It is a long journey and in my view should be, without short cuts. It is not a matter of 'getting qualifications and notching up hours' per se, but having enough experience of a wide range of helping relationships to form a thorough knowledge of social systems and really absorb and understand the dynamics of individual relationships.

Comment
With one degree, three postgraduate diplomas, three further major training courses, at least 10 years of in-service training and accreditation with both counselling and psychotherapy associations, Sheena is probably the most qualified of all my case studies. Paradoxically she is not overly impressed with obtaining qualifications but is

certainly a devotee of putting together the widest possible range of learning and practical experiences.

Conclusions

At the time of writing the issue of rationing of health care, not for the first time, is being debated in the press and the major political parties are setting out there stalls for the 1997 general election. It is claimed that there always has been rationing in the NHS and will increasingly be so in future as expectations and demand rise. The question is how to ration services and it is within this context that counselling will have to compete for scarce resources and justify its place. Fortunately research is showing that counselling is not only popular but potentially good value for money and therefore it is poised to become the next established and recognised paramedical profession. Growth of jobs is likely in secondary care, related community projects, and also in primary care although in the latter they may be moderately paid and part time.

CHAPTER 4:
WORK RELATED COUNSELLING

"Post trauma counselling? I'd rather go down the pub with my mates." Tony Bullimore, lone yachtsman and survivor.

Introduction

Work related counselling both inside and outside the workplace is expanding. Organisations and their individual employees are increasingly being asked to re-define themselves, often quite radically, and with this trend there is a specific and spreading area of counselling being shaped around fast-changing workplaces attempting to deal with areas of distress. These areas range from redundancy, disaster trauma and bereavement to bullying and harassment at work. Melanie Child (1994) argues that the tougher things are at the workplace then the more there is a need to pick up the pieces, and this is supported by Dunn (1994) who notes that the last decade has seen a sharp increase in both the speed and complexity of change in the workplace. He says that workplace counselling is therefore assuming increased importance as a management tool. According to two recent surveys by MORI 93% of the workforce support counselling services provided by employers. However, only 48% of employees in organisations with over 50 staff have access to counselling, with a better record in the public sector. Child advocates pro-active counselling skills applied by trusted colleagues or other experts, and in-house, or an external counselling service, or Employee Assistance Programmes (EAPs).

"Suit wars"

This issue of the management of rapid change is by no means restricted to industry and commerce. Many university staff have been struggling to adjust to big increases in student/staff ratios, plus pressure to do research, attract external funds, and the monitoring of their teaching performance. Then along came the Enterprise in Higher Education Initiative which brought with it further changes towards student centred learning, increased emphasis on students developing transferable skills, and a fundamental review of pastoral care. In universities and other large organisations it is now common for stress levels to be monitored and appropriate action taken: that action may include counselling.

Stress and Depression

Child (1994) describes workshops on stress as an acceptable form of psychological damage limitation, especially when they are run in conjunction with a confidential counselling service. Hopkins (1994) accounts for the growth in stress by economic uncertainty, ever more competitive markets, job losses, performance-related targets, new skill requirements and unprecedented change. She argues that stress at work is caused by a complicated combination of both personal and work-related issues and, in order to be really effective, counselling programmes at work must address both. Burrell and Levy (1995) report a growing number of incidents called 'work rage' and, according to Cary Cooper, professor of organisational psychology at UMIST, 'suit wars' were prompted by job cuts and an efficiency drive that had transformed the office environment. Hopkins (1994) also notes that organisations may be looking for a 'quick fix' and there may be no real wish or intention on the part of the organisation to change. In this case the correct thing is for the counselling provider to courageously walk away.

"We should not be providing 'sticking plaster' or 'laundry baskets'" (Hopkins 1994: 14)

Dunn (1994) goes further in asserting that counselling is overtaking training as a means of generating improvements in performance in a fast changing environment. He states bluntly that two out of three counselling sessions are used to reduce stress (four out five in the public sector). However, less than half the line managers in the MORI survey had received any kind of training in counselling techniques, although organisations are apparently now beginning to invest heavily in providing counselling services, either by using outside experts or by training their own staff. A few remain to be convinced:–

"Being stressed is being important . . . somehow stress, like ME or dyslexia, has become a bizarrely aspirational ailment. The truly ambitious even manage to have children whose school-work is not up to scratch because at five the kids are feeling the pressure. Truly, the stressed-out shall inherit the earth." (Moore: 1995)

Moore suggests that the greatest stress is life lived in grinding poverty, rather than 'a mark of millennial superiority' but Dunn strikes an optimistic note with the MORI surveys showing that 90% of British organisations expect to obtain direct bottom-line benefits from counselling services, in terms of reduced absenteeism and more efficient performance. I am reminded of how the attitude towards student counselling is similarly becoming more positive in universities as they face up to the fact that they will be penalised if they display high drop-out rates. I have always felt positive about counselling and I see no harm in this work being subject not only to success criteria but also value for money criteria.

"Being stressed is being important"

Macwhinnie (1994) points out the staggering annual £3.5 billion cost of depression, including 155 million days lost at work. She argues that, although work has a largely beneficial impact on mental health, there are circumstances which can trigger an employee's depression such as working in isolation (a potential problem for counsellors), insensitive redundancy procedures, unrealistic productivity demands, bullying, and inadequate skills for a task. She sees the onus increasingly on employers to implement an appropriate policy and notes that more companies are being sued by employees for stress-related illnesses. Like Child she advocates a pro-active approach which includes workplace counselling as a cornerstone of company policy.

Employee Assistance Programmes

According to Galliano there has been considerable growth in the the number of companies using EAPs. The UK Employee Assistance Professionals Association defines an EAP as:–

"the provision of counselling and other support services for the employees who are distracted by personal concerns including stress, relationships, family, alcohol, drugs, financial, legal and other issues. It further defines it as a programme to assist the organisation in the identification and amelioration of productivity issues in employees adversely affected by personal concerns." (Galliano 1994: 13)

Typically EAP providers aim to work with counsellors who ideally have BAC accreditation, have at least two years continuously supervised work, routinely attend training courses, and consult in rooms solely for that purpose. Freelance counsellors should have several years of private practice and evidence of current indemnity and public liability cover. EAP providers pay around £30 per session to counsellors in private practice who form part of their referral network, some of whom are practicing from rooms in their own homes. Short term assistance will be offered (maximum eight sessions) and much counselling is conducted by telephone. Companies will ultimately want to see benefits being created for the organisation: however, all EAPs are confidential and counsellors are accountable to them, not others.

As many as 600 freelance counsellors are working for specialist EAP companies and Galliano reckons the EAP movement has only just begun. This is in line with the forecast of counselling course leaders in my own survey who identified medical and *work* settings as far more likely to grow than others, and stress as a growing presenting concern. However, these opportunities will only be open to individuals who can satisfy the training, professional and business requirements being demanded by EAP providers and their customer organisations. Some of the main companies are ICAS, FOCUS, Care Assist and Mentors. So it is clear that counselling at work lends itself to linking into private practice and there is great potential for selling services to large companies. What seems to me to be of enormous and encouraging significance is that many companies are beginning to realise that economic growth depends as much on staff well-being as on rationalisation or new technology.

A Range of Services

A wide variety of companies use internal or external counsellors such as Shell UK, W H Smith, Royal College of Nursing, Midland Bank, British Airways, the BBC and also many Government departments, police forces etc. Tehrani (1995) describes a comprehensive health and support service but stresses that only around 5% of employees are assessed as needing counselling, which is itself likely to be flexible, pragmatic and short term. The strategies in her large organisation include educational factsheets and seminars, life-style advice and guidance, individual and environmental stress assessments, relaxation training and advice to managers on the reduction of social and psychological stressors within the workplace. She points out that health and safety legislation requires employers to ensure the good health, including mental health, of their workforce and Mr. John Walker is the first person in the UK to successfully sue his employer for work related stress. In a famous ruling in 1996 some West Yorkshire police officers won their case on appeal for compensation for stress related illness arising from the Hillsborough stadium disaster.

Astonishingly Cooper (1994) showed that of counsellors from EAPs 11% had had no formal counselling qualification and a further 11% only possessed a basic certificate. Tehrani (1995) points out that guidelines for EAPs (EAPA 1995) provide useful hints for counsellors but fail to establish competency standards, disciplinary codes, qualifications or enforceable standards of practice for its members. Organisational counsellors are regularly put into positions where they are expected to handle the competing needs and demands of an employee, a manager and the organisation simultaneously. Even an accredited or chartered counsellor may not have the necessary training and experience of working in a particular setting in order to be competent. Furthermore, it transpires that many counselling supervisors have had no training for that role which seems strange in a profession that puts so much faith in supervision. The overall cost of an internal service will be £50-60 per hour but this could be less than the true costs of an inadequate service when account is taken of sickness absence, medical retirements and the risk of expensive litigation.

The following might be typical of an employer responding positively to the need for staff counselling. This is the advert which appeared recently in the weekly staff bulletin of a large accountancy firm:–

"**Do You Want To Talk?**

As the pressures of combining a demanding workload with a busy personal life increase you may feel worried, anxious or simply demotivated. Many people have found that talking to someone who is independent can help. For some it is a chance to let off steam, others may need advice, a few people want someone to mediate between them and a supervisor. All discussions are confidential and can take place at any time and in any location . . . any action that takes place will be because you wanted it to and no records are kept of our meeting. If you feel you want someone to listen please telephone me on xxxx or call into the Personnel reception at any time and ask for me, Claire, ext. xxxx, Assistant Personnel Officer (Equal Opportunities and Welfare)"

When Claire was appointed in 1993 about one third of her work was expected to be welfare (including staff counselling), plus equal opportunities and general personnel work. By late 1994 she was seeing one new person per week on average plus others for several sessions. She was also involved in the working party follow-up to the company doctor's stress survey. Her training and qualifications include Institute of Personnel Management (IPM) Stage 1 and approximately ten days training in counselling led by personnel consultants. She refers clients when necessary but does not have supervision. She plans to undertake more counselling training and is confident that she is suited to staff counselling work. However, she is not a 'counsellor' and I am doubtful of the wisdom of taking on regular clients especially unsupervised.

Post Trauma Counselling

There has been a large increase in the number of counsellors doing post trauma counselling and debriefing after critical incidents, assaults, robberies and so on. For example, victim support groups are one of the most recently created counselling and helping organisations doing sterling voluntary work with the casualties of crime. Tehrani (1995) notes that there have been some large awards of compensation payments to employees suffering from Post Traumatic Stress Disorder (PTSD), such as £5 million for the survivors of the Ocean Odyssey oil rig. Violence in the workplace may be on the increase, especially in pubs, clubs, betting shops and off-licenses as well as traditional targets such as banks and building societies. Reactions include anxiety, paranoia and depression and employers are recognising the importance of offering post incident support (PIS) to their staff. One group of off-licenses regards an expenditure of £20,000pa as good value because it reduces staff illness and absenteeism and boosts morale. PIS is either run in-house, for example by sending area managers for specialist training, or by a combination of an internal team and an outside agency such as an EAP. A fast response can be made but no attempt is made to force anything on the employee.

The Herald of Free Enterprise (sea), the Clapham Junction disaster (rail) and, most infamous of all, the Lockerbie disaster (air) brought out the crisis counsellors in force. The day after a hooded gunman stabbed a twelve year old girl to death at Hall Garth school in April 1994, a team of educational psychologists and social workers were installed in the staffroom. Counselling has also been offered both to members of the jury and to journalists reporting the trial of Rosemary West (who was convicted of ten grisly cases of murder of girls and young women), and even national lottery winners, a novel form of 'disaster'! The need for this specialised counselling has been challenged by some commentators such as Lightfoot (1994):—

' "Counsellors have by stealth become yet another emergency service. Their presence has become routine at all disasters though there is little evidence that people shocked to the core with grief, disbelief and denial find them anything but a distraction. . . . It is, perhaps, a sign of the times that professional helpers are now taking over the role previously performed by family, friends, neighbours or the churches." (Sunday Times 3rd April 1994)

One crisis centre which specialises in psychological trauma states that trauma can prevent perfectly heathy people from working normally and can seriously affect their personal lives. Since 1985 it claims unique experience of working with major disasters and has developed treatment methods which help to eliminate disturbing symptoms. These methods aim to give people information about what they are experiencing, the confidence to communicate, greater control over their symptoms and reassurance that they will win through. This centre has trained many crisis support teams for Social Service Departments, Health Authorities and Emergency Services to deal with the aftermath of major incidents and sees the attitude of senior management (often poor) as a key element in dealing with trauma in the workplace. The centre focuses primarily on acute stress arising out of traumatic incidents and the prevention of chronic stress problems, with group debriefing seen as the most useful and cost effective way of working with staff trauma. I am interested to note that it is deliberately described as 'debriefing' rather than 'counselling' in order to avoid unnecessary stigma.

There is no doubt that people who are clearly *not* recovering long after the death of a loved one or traumatic event do need specialist help, and there is no doubt in my mind of the value of such specialist counsellors. However, there are obvious dangers in rushing to send in an army of possibly inadequately trained counsellors who may be tempted to fit all victims to the relevant theory. Some survivors have reported their exasperation with counsellors who seem determined to identify and label these survivors' guilt. Lightfoot (1994) quoted one relieved survivor who resorted to hiding behind the curtains when her counsellor came to call for the fifth time. As in the pastoral care setting, there is a danger that the client has been pressured to engage in counselling. There may be occasions when you feel that the professional thing to do is to courageously walk away from the situation. However, the bereavement counsellors I have spoken to readily agree that their work is complimentary to, and in no sense a replacement for, the love and support of friends and relations.

Training

There are relatively few courses dedicated to training for counselling in work settings although these are expanding. A few examples at advanced level are listed in the 1996 BAC Training Directory:–

i   Bristol University. Diploma in Counselling at Work.

ii   Edge Hill College of FE, Ormskirk. Postgraduate Diploma in Counselling Skills and Approaches in Professional Settings.

iii Roehampton Institute, London, with TDA Consulting. Cert/Diploma in Counselling at Work.

Introductory courses include:–

i   Birmingham University. Certificate in Counselling at Work.

ii   Rotherham College of Arts and Technology. Counselling Skills in The Workplace.

iii Tavistock Institute of Marital Studies, London. Thinking and Acting: Staff Supervision.

iv   ICAS, Milton Keynes. Counselling Skills at Work.

The IPD will have an up to date list of their approved courses which will include counselling.

A Week in the Life of Kimberley (39), a Newly Self-employed Work-related Counsellor

Monday am	Visit to an accountant to understand implications of self employment and tax self-assessment (system introduced in April 1997).
Monday pm	Prepare leaflets and business cards. Follow up any queries – fast.
Tuesday am	See three clients (all referred by word of mouth) in newly hired consulting rooms.
Tuesday pm	Visit conference venue where workshops may be run in the future. Carry on with administration. Follow up phone calls – fast.
Wednesday	Attend one-day workshop on "Setting up on your own". Use opportunity to make like-minded contacts. (Keep in touch with them).
Thursday	Fill in application form to become associate counsellor for an EAP provider, including two case studies – time consuming. Send out two leaflets and short letters to contacts who have shown interest. Try cold calling organisations known to be undergoing change. Send follow up paperwork immediately.
Friday am	Supervision session. Prepare advertisement for Association for Counselling at Work and for IPD journal. Adjust business plan. Call business advice centre.
Friday pm.	Prepare outline for stress workshop to be run following month. Tackle next stage of BAC Accreditation application (time consuming). Apply rules of workshop to self!

It can be an exciting but also unnerving experience at the beginning of self-employment unless it has been thought through and there is a certain amount of finance to provide income in the early uncertain months. The above week demonstrates the need for self-sufficiency and discipline, and also the ability to put yourself forward. In general, if you are able to establish a good reputation, and this may take six months to a year of concentrated effort, the work is likely to come in without such energy needed in the above timetable. Some of you may find it very hard to market yourselves, as it will be a very different experience from being under the umbrella of a counselling agency.

At the beginning it is important to set realistic expectations and to build in a support network which will see you through the uncertainties. Take time to consider whether you have the right qualities to enjoy the benefits of self-employment:– for example, the freedom to work in your own style to your own standards, and a degree of flexibility in time management. The time flexibility can work both ways and at at high peaks there is a genuine danger of not switching off, especially if your office is located at home. You need to have determination, initiative and an attitude which will ensure that you set yourself high professional standards. Above all must be the capacity to balance energy and patience, to blend imagination, creativity and reality, and to be clear about what you can and what you cannot offer to your clients.

Typical Jobs
1 OCCUPATIONAL HEALTH COUNSELLOR (Local Authority)
Service Criteria
1 Provide a confidential counselling service to staff.

2 Counsel people across a range of problems including work-related, family, substance misuse, bereavement, crime etc.

3 Referrals by departmental staffing officers.

4 Counselling contract includes an initial assessment session followed by up to six sessions.

5 In the initial assessment session counsellors will identify presenting concern, obtain relevant history, collaborate on devising strategies for resolving problems, determine whether short-term counselling is appropriate and agree dates.

6 The council will brief the counsellor on relevant work issues or organisational developments.

7 Counsellors provide information on accommodation, including suitability for access for people with disabilities. Counsellor and client might mutually agree to meet in council premises.

8 Within seven days counsellors must be available for an initial session, and arrange further sessions to start within another 14 days.

There are further guidelines on equality of opportunity, confidentiality, feedback (qualitative and quantitative every six months) and fees (to be tendered).

Criteria for Counsellor Selection

Essential Prerequisites:–
1 Appropriately qualified and experienced (BAC, UKCP or equivalent)
2 Currently in supervision.

Essential Characteristics:-
- Non-judgmental, non-possessively warm, prize any client equal.
- Advanced, accurate empathy.
- Genuine, congruent and transparent with their feelings.
- Highly self-aware and able to manage own feelings.
- Emotionally stable and working on their personal growth.
- Capacity to avoid becoming emotionally involved with clients.

Essential Competencies:– These include communication skills, active listening, paraphrasing and summarizing skills, empathy, articulacy, structuring skills (eg. goal-setting, negotiating), ability to confront and challenge, cope with distress, self disclose, maintain records, deal with transference and counter- transference, and organisational skills.

Essential knowledge includes theories, techniques, relevant law, equal opportunities, clients' social conditions, relevant cultural backgrounds and behavioural norms, ethics and issues of power and oppression.

Tender Application Form

Personal details, qualifications, training; relevant counselling experience; how you apply the code of ethics; supervision arrangements; BAC or UKCP listed?

How would you want to familiarise yourself with the organisation , culture and values of the Authority?
Please provide detailed arrangements of your fee structure (successful candidates will have opportunity to discuss).
Please describe what you understand by equal opportunities in provision of a counselling service.
List your specialist areas of counselling.
Write on one side of A4 how you would respond to each of the following three scenarios:-
1 A middle manager under-achieving, missing many days with various ailments, engaged in an inappropriate relationship with a junior.
2 An administration assistant having panic attacks at work who reveals a problem of dependency on sleeping pills and alcohol.
3 An Asian female housing officer suffering from abuse from an angry tenant in arrears.

2 COUNSELLOR WITH AN EAP PROVIDER

Job Purpose

To ensure the provision of an efficient Employee Assistant Programme operating on a 24 hour, 365 day basis in accordance with professional, ethical and company standards.

Knowledge and Skills Required

1 Acknowledged counselling qualification and relevant experience.
2 BAC full membership.
3 Seasoned ability.
4 Understanding ethical and confidentiality standards of a telephone counselling service.
5 Understanding company counselling services and sub-contractor requirements.
6 Understanding rota, call-logging and programme records.
7 Professional team member.
8 Establish relationships and peer support.
9 Presentational, social, oral and communication skills.
10 Commercial awareness.

Principal Accountabilities

These include provision of high standard telephone counselling service, ability to facilitate referral for face-to-face counselling where appropriate, visit associate counsellors, contribute to rota duties including 'out of hours', produce articles and associated product, represent service and company, participate in supervision sessions, maintain records, and compile and renew database.

Application Form

Personal details; education and training; membership of associations, foreign languages; employment history and period of notice; expected salary range, willingness to work overtime and weekends; any other commitments.

Please give details of any experience/qualifications or achievement which you feel may be relevant.

3 OCCUPATIONAL HEALTH WELFARE COUNSELLOR (Police Force)

Job Description

Job title:– Occupational Health Welfare Counsellor; Pay £16,208-£20,481; 41 hours pw (including lunch breaks).

Purpose:– Part of multi-disciplinary team to prevent illness through work activity and promote health, safety and well-being of personnel. Provide a confidential counselling, support and information service to staff and their families.

Key Responsibilities

Deliver trauma support programme; counselling, support and information to individuals, couples and groups; provide information, and welfare guidance to line managers; maintain case notes, prepare reports and write letters on behalf of clients; support 24 hour emergency rota; give presentations to groups to promote and explain role of service; maintain high level of expertise and adhere to code of ethics.

Qualifications and Experience

BAC equivalent; application of a range of counselling theories and methods; awareness of external referral agencies and support systems.

Application Form

Personal and family details (including parents and partners); employment history (including reasons for leaving); achievements (education, career, awards, prizes); interests (including voluntary work); details of Armed Service Reserve, health, convictions (!) and financial standing.

State why you consider that you are particularly suited to this position and what you can contribute to the post if appointed.

Case Study of a Comparative Newcomer :– Stephanie (early forties)
Work Experience

1993	Consultancy Group:– Career path mapping, personal redundancy and outplacement work with managers at a mid-life and mid-career stage.
	University:– Career counselling.
1994	Selector for Voluntary Work Organisation.
1994	Bereavement Counsellor with Voluntary Organisation.
1991-93	Personnel Officer (Publisher).
1988-90	Deputy Director (British Council, North Africa).
1985-88	Overseas Personnel Officer (Charity).
1980-85	Assistant Registrar (Retailer).
1976-80	Temporary contracts organising volunteer programme with Voluntary Organisation, and managing opinion surveys with Computer Company.
1974-76	English Teacher (secondary school, Tanzania).

Education and Qualifications

1995	Diploma in Counselling (university).
1994	Cert. in Counselling (university).
1991	Cert. in Counselling Skills (independent counselling organisation).
1991	Course of 10 Sessions in Bereavement Counselling (charity).
1995	Myers Briggs Type Indicator Qualifying Workshop.
1986	Aptitude Testing Cert.
1981-84	Membership of the Institute of Personnel and Development.
1974	BA (hons.) in Psychology (university).

The Job(s)

1 Redundancy counsellor (one or two days per week); Salary £250 per day working for a consultancy group. Currently seeing eight clients per week, some for one session per week for up to 18 months, and others for eight sessions of 2.5 hours per week in a group. Some of the work is with the 'survivors' of downsizing who suffer from guilt. Also qualified to give psychometric test feedback to clients of another consultant. I survived when ten consultants were reduced to three!

2 Careers counsellor in a Scottish University (half time); Salary £10, 200 pa. (plus 3 & 4 – Selector for voluntary organisation, and bereavement counselling).

Selection Procedures
1 Speculative Application with CV, followed by three interviews with separate individuals.
2 Two Panel Interviews.

Household Context
Single Parent with one young son at time of making major career decisions. Now with salaried partner.

Satisfactions
1 It is exciting work when clients successfully turn their lives around: the 'before' and 'after' situations are often very satisfying.
2 The two jobs complement each other, with poor students at the start or early stages of their careers and others at mid and/or later stages.
3 Turning from gamekeeper (personnel) to poacher (counsellor).

Disappointments
Lack of university funding for some of the more creative training courses.

Surprises
Cramped physical conditions at university.

Lucky Breaks
Being able to secure half time work plus consultancy.

The Future
Developing expertise and experience within the context of personal and/or career counselling.

Advice
Find a balance which feels comfortable between formal learning and counselling experience, but try to keep up with both areas.

Comment
Stephanie is clearly an adventurer and something of a risk taker. She was determined to take the half time careers job when she knew that she could not possibly manage on that salary alone and it was quite some time before she was offered the consultancy work. Her professionalism has been a significant factor in her progress to date:– obtaining the most appropriate qualifications and undergoing approved training courses. BAC accreditation is only a matter of time. Her versatility, broadly based experience and qualifications will enable her to hedge her bets in an uncertain world.

Case study of a High Flyer:– Jerome
Work Experience
1991	Partner in Smith and Jones.
1989-91	Self employed counsellor, supervisor of counselling and facilitator on workshops and seminars in the workplace.
1987-89	Employee counsellor: telephone and face to face.
1978-81	Relationships counsellor.

Counselling Training
1995	Diploma in Family Therapy.
1994-95	Family Systems Certificate.

1989-90   Diploma in Counselling and Supervision.
1979-81   Marriage Guidance Training.
                Also numerous short courses such as post traumatic stress disorder,
                sexual abuse, HIV/AIDS, stress management, group dynamics,
                training for trainers, solution focussed brief therapy.
1993   Ongoing therapy.

The Job
Partnership:– providers of confidential counselling and related training and workshops
to organisations.

Selection Process
Both previously worked for an EAP. Victoria set the company up in 1990 and then it
became a partnership in 1992.

Household Context
Married salaried partner, three grown up children and one dependent dog.

Satisfactions
The variety of the job is exciting: working in many different contexts from workplace
to In and Outpatient psychiatric unit as well as management training.

Disappointments
Hopeless at delegation and therefore get bogged down with all the administration.

Surprises
Constantly flattered by the offers of different kinds of work that seem to value the input of
someone experienced in counselling from in-patient treatment to management consultancy.

Lucky Breaks
Confronting a psychiatrist after a seminar and he offered me a post as an honorary
therapist. Joining the Association for Counselling at Work as I got my job as an employee
counsellor through the networking.

The Future
To be involved in counselling as it becomes more part of management in business. To
be recognised as a member of a professional body as a counsellor that is to be
accredited or a member of the forthcoming Register of Counsellors.

Advice for Budding Partners
Sit at the front of all the seminars, workshops and conferences you go to. Try to gain
experience of the area you are working in that does not include counselling: eg I took
a Certificate in Personnel Practice to help my understanding of the workplace. The
development of my counselling career has broadened my horizons, brought me into
contact with wonderful 'human' people from whom I am continually learning, both
clients and colleagues.

Conclusions
Employee counselling is an expanding field and full of opportunities. Interested readers
might contact large companies or major EAP providers or consider tendering for
such work themselves, although it is necessary to be commercially knowledgeable.
The work is often better paid than in other sectors, for example one EAP provider
pays its counsellors in London £200 per day. Marketing and presentation skills are
important in securing such business and these are not exactly core skills in counselling.

However, counselling by established staff is actually valued by employers in the region of £30 per hour when account is taken of overheads (space, lighting, insurance etc) as well as salaries, and the pressure is mounting to justify the existence of services in terms of value for money. Gone are the days when the service, in both public and commercial sectors, was there because it was there and presumed to be doing good work. The real differences between employed and freelance counselling are therefore not as great as you might think.

CHAPTER 5:
COUNSELLING IN EDUCATIONAL SETTINGS

Introduction

Within the state education system growth and development of counselling has been heavily concentrated in the further and higher education sectors, with over 3,000 members in that division of BAC in 1996. This is roughly double the number in the counselling in schools division which makes the latter the second smallest (the Race division has about 600 members). Funding of a universal system of counselling in the primary and secondary sectors has never got off the ground largely because of the structure of the existing education welfare system which is monopolized by the educational psychologists and educational welfare officers.

The growth in training and further and higher education and related reforms have resulted in very rapid growth in membership of the Association of Student Counsellors (ASC). Major developments in the 1990s which have important implications for counselling and related work include the aim that one in three young people should enter higher education by the year 2000, the drive to recruit a wider range of students (notably older people and ethnic minorities), and finally the rapid increase in the numbers of full fee paying international students. This was recently described to me by a senior colleague as a 'lurch to mass higher education' against a background of worsening student/staff ratios and increasingly stringent budgets.

Schools

Klinefelter (1994) describes a pilot project set up and funded by the health authority, for three counsellors to work with students, parents and teachers in six schools to provide therapeutic counselling for people in schools. The counsellors had a combination of counselling experience with young people and a knowledge of the secondary education system. To ensure that the student is understood within the social context teachers, parents and other family members are frequently included in the counselling and Klinefelter stresses the importance of the counsellor not being seen to be taking sides.

Students are seen for up to ten sessions and where longer term counselling is indicated a referral to the appropriate mental health service is made. Students were normally seen within two weeks of referral and the range of presenting concerns included self esteem, bullying, peer problems, and family problems such as redundancy, alcoholism and bereavement. The service saw 282 students in 1992/3 and 449 (212 boys and 237 girls) in 1993/4, an increase of nearly 60%. The service was extended to two primary schools on a regular basis and 20 others occasionally. Klinefelter concludes that the service has received positive support from students, teachers, parents and community agencies, with the most significant indicator of success being the continued funding.

However, I am not aware of any evidence that there is likely to be significant growth of counselling in schools. The decision to extend the above service means that there is reckoned to be good value for money but there are competing claims for *health or social services* and it is highly unlikely that the resources could be found from an *education* budget. At the time of writing the first school to be closed, on the alleged grounds of failing their students, has been announced in a blaze of publicity, and violence in schools looks set to be a major issue in the 1997 general election. Resources may well be directed at counselling parents if not children. There may well be growth in the private school sector because, although the schools may be reticent about highlighting the fact that there are problems, this has not inhibited many of them from appointing counsellors, usually on a part time basis.

Further and Higher Education

FE colleges have increasingly adopted a strategy of customer friendly service with the aim of increasing student numbers and minimising drop-out rates. An extreme example is the college which has built a combined nursery and dependent relative centre for the benefit of their mature students. One effect has been for student services departments to embrace everything from publicity to progression and one of the new universities has followed this trend by taking over admissions. Unhappily for FE colleges high dropout rates have been announced in late 1996 on the new GNVQ courses which may result in financial penalties, especially for those courses with the poorest results. However, with a New Labour 'Government in waiting' promising to eliminate youth unemployment, further growth and change seems likely in further education and this could well mean more jobs in counselling and guidance work.

It is a reflection of their relative autonomy that university counselling services vary considerably in the UK in terms of both size and structure. For example two universities recently advertised for student counsellors and only 'psychotherapists' and 'person centred counsellors' respectively need apply. I myself trained in an old university where counselling was located in a student health service dominated by doctors and clinical psychologists. Most of the newer universities (ie former polytechnics) have adopted a unified approach to service provision and their heads have formed an effective political lobby through their Association of Managers of Student Services in Higher Education (AMOSSHE). The old universities have tended to have a more fragmented structure with counselling and careers services usually separate and with different philosophies.

Government funding for universities is in the process of being linked directly to drop-out rates. The census date for student is, significantly, being changed from November to the following July which gives universities a real incentive to hang on to their students until the end of the academic year. This cuts both ways for counsellors in the sense that effective trouble shooting will bring financial benefits to the institution but this could compromise the counsellor's role. It might be in a student's best interests to leave earlier than the end of the academic year, for example within six months of starting in order to safeguard future grant entitlement.

The training of counsellors is normally seen to be holistic but, such is the complexity of contemporary society and the wide range of problems encountered, that there are forces working towards specialization, especially in higher education. In the 1980s several universities had integrated careers and counselling services which dealt with literally any concern presented by any student. Within a single working day a counsellor might encounter the following:– depression over broken relationship, a final year student clueless about careers, problems with a work permit, a disciplinary hearing for alleged cheating, examination anxiety, essay writing problems (possible dyslexia), and a draft application form for British Airways. By the mid 1990s the scene had changed dramatically as shown in table 1 for a university in the Midlands.

TABLE 1: COUNSELLING AND ADVISORY POSTS

1981	1997
Student Services	**Student Services**
Student Counsellors (2.5)	Student Counsellors (1.5)
(all issues)	Careers Counsellors (3.5)
	International Students Advisors (1.7)
	Mature Students Advisor (0.5)
	Dyslexic Students Advisor (0.2)
	Disabled Students Advisor (0.5)
	General Practice
	Practice counsellor (1.0 equiv.)
	Finance Department
	Financial Advisors (2.6)
	(loans, hardship fund)
	Students Union
	Advice Workers (2.5)
	(including debt counselling)
Grand Total 2.5 posts	**Grand Total (in 4 deptartments) 14.0 posts** (9 full time, 10 part time)

Nine of the above 19 staff have obtained or are studying for an advanced counselling qualification and the rest all have some counselling training. Even allowing for the substantial growth in student numbers, counselling and advisory posts over these thirteen years have increased significantly in real terms. Much as counsellors may have enjoyed the variety and challenge of the early 1980s those I have spoken to admit that specialization has been desirable and, significantly, no British university has retained integrated counselling, careers and financial advisory services. Oxford Brookes is an example of a university that has invested heavily in high quality student services, including careers counselling and educational guidance, which may help to explain why OBU came top of the new universities in the 1996 Sunday Times league table.

Responding to the Whole Student Experience

Student services managers have identified the need to respond to the 'whole student experience' and most have decided on a policy of having counsellors who lead in the specialist areas of international students, mature students and so on. One university recently advertised for a black counsellor and another for an 'educational counsellor' for which they required a qualified counsellor with specialist interests in the field of study behaviour. I know of mature student and international student advisors who are being subsidized by their employers to train in counselling at least to certificate level. In some universities counsellors are acting as consultants and trainers to a new breed of personal tutors who are given a reduced teaching load in order to perform a wider role of pastoral care. Many organisations with limited resources have staff who function interchangeably as counsellors, advisors, advocates and so on so it certainly helps to be versatile. I find these reforms exciting but not all agree with me.

The Association of Graduate Recruiters (1995) have called for 'seamless careers guidance' at school and beyond for, ideally, a new breed of self reliant student. Several universities do now build library and study skills into first year courses, and some offer careers education within the curriculum. This reflects a fresh emphasis on 'process' which empowers students to plan and manage the complex and potentially stressful transition to the world of work, and to switch the overall emphasis from knowledge acquisition to skill development. Paradoxically the less and less money students receive directly from the taxpayer in grants the more they can expect demonstrably high standards of pastoral care and support services and this could mean more jobs in guidance and counselling. Some tension has been discerned between student services managers and ASC with the former arguing that counselling has to move towards short term focussed work, which includes all the issues affecting student learning including welfare (eg finance and benefit entitlement). There are still student counsellors who state that they are psychotherapists who just happen to work in higher education, but my own forecast is that it will become increasingly difficult for counselling services in both further and higher education to engage in long term work.

Given the growth and change in counselling in education I am surprised that there is only one advanced course which is devoted to educational settings:- London University (Institute of Education) Diploma in Pastoral Care and Personal Social Education. However, there are three courses in Guidance and Counselling Adults at Luton, Northumbria, and Ulster Universities and there is a course in Applied Advice Work at South Bank University.

A Day in the Life of Madge (45, Student Counsellor, College of Higher Education)

9 am   Time to go through the post, look at the diary (full, as usual except for an emergency slot at 3 00 pm) and get out my notes (very brief) for the students I have seen before.

9.30   **Carol**, is a mature student in her late thirties and her worries about her habitually poor exam performance have reached crisis proportions. A key ingredient in the process whereby she winds herself up seems to be her fantasy about what examiners expect — namely a coherent, elegant demonstration of superb insights. Here I find it helpful to bring into play my own experience as a tutor, namely that at this level (BA) examiners are primarily concerned with straightforward demonstrations of some understanding. I explain how I have even given pass grades to students who, clearly running out of time, produce a check list of comments which clearly demonstrate reasonable understanding of subject. She is surprised and relieved.

"examinated anxiety"

10.30   **Tom** is my longest running client ever and is now in his third year. His original presenting concern was a disastrous relationship with parents and an acute sense of loneliness at college. Originally very confused about his sexual orientation, he has recently started an intense gay relationship with a much older man. He insists on going into graphic details of his new found sex life which makes me feel like a voyeur (it is even worse when I am dealing with lesbians with whom I find it helpful to 'translate' into heterosexual experience). His new found confidence is coming over as arrogance and I toy with the idea of pointing this out to him. Just time for a quick coffee.

11.30   **Lisa** I have not seen since enrolment week when she was devastated to discover she had been labelled an 'academic failure'. A complex picture emerged based on the minimum three module pass rule and together we devise an elaborate plot, involving possible retrospective elimination of term three on medical grounds (Lisa will discuss this with her GP) and supportive reports from a sympathetic tutor and myself.

I attend a lunchtime staff meeting to discuss the proposed 'tax free pay' scheme. This turns out to be a bizarre but perfectly legal scheme in which the college and employees who opt in both save money. I shall be £300 a year better off! I bump into the assistant dean and clarify the circumstances in which they can bend the three module pass rule. Back in my office I field a call from a tutor anxious to know whether I have seen a student called Sarah (I have). I patiently explain that the fact that she might be seeing me is itself confidential. He seems very bothered and from what Sarah has been telling me I have a fair idea why (they have been sleeping together).

2 00   **Carla** arrives late and harassed as usual. I know I shouldn't have favourite clients but Carla is one of them because our encounters are invariably lively albeit exasperating. Carla was recently in the local hospital self harm unit after an alleged overdose. One of the nurse therapists in the unit had commented to me afterwards how much Carla reminded her of an operatic (tragic) heroine, with me playing a supporting role as I sat on the bed holding her hand (I don't often touch clients). We discuss, with much anguish and some laughter, the latest row with her semi-impotent boyfriend.

3.00   **Jim** has been booked as an emergency. He is reeking of alcohol so initially I have to decide whether to talk to him at all, but as he is reasonably coherent I carry on. Jim is a mature student with a serious alcohol problem. He had performed heroics in passing last year's access course and managed to stay sober, but was immediately out of his depth on a degree course partly because of a poor choice of fields . He has already spent this term's grant and his wife is threatening to throw him out. My heart sinks when he asserts that he will be able, with help from me, to revert to moderate 'social drinking' and he will solve his financial problems by securing sponsorship from Sainsbury's. Both of these are fantasies nurtured by five pints in the union bar. With his permission, I arrange an appointment with my careers advisor colleague Graham, a tough but sympathetic character with some experience of drink problems. Between us we might be able to help Jim but he looks to me like one who is not suited to higher education.

"Jim, not suited to HE"

4.00   I am now running late which I hate but **Ben** doesn't mind, being one of the most apathetic and yet amiable students I have ever met. He started seeing me in week 4 (it's now week 8) because he was missing many classes and falling behind with coursework. I had leapt at the opportunity to try out a cognitive-behavioural approach, focussing on facts such as Ben missing his evening practical class mainly because of watching TV. By the time 'Neighbours' was over he couldn't resist the news and so the evening wore on, watching a series of programmes of little real interest. In spite of his compliant attitude and desire to please our progress has been zero. I try a different tack – "are you actually *interested* in geology Ben"? "No"he replies in his usual laid back style, "not at all actually". I had, not for the first time, overlooked the obvious! We go back to basics and it transpires Ben is only at college at all to please his anxious single parent mother. Some time after he's gone I roar with laughter, which is not a bad way to end the day. Correspondence and administration take me up to 5.30.

Typical Jobs
1   Mature Student Advisor (Half time temporary for two years, University)
Purpose of Job:- The university wishes to attract more mature and ethnic minority students, via access courses and other means. The mature student advisor will offer a specialist service for those who are experiencing particular difficulties in coping with academic work. Much of the work will be pro-active:– liaising with staff and students in order to discover how best to promote effective study behaviour. After two years the effectiveness of this new appointment will be evaluated.

Job Requirements
1 Education to graduate and preferably higher degree standard.
2 Knowledge of and enthusiasm for equal opportunities.
3 Ability to empathize with a wide range of clients.
4 A relevant qualification such as teaching, counselling or careers guidance.
5 Knowledge and experience of study skills training.
6 Interviewing, teamwork and presentation skills.

Application Form
Personal Details; Current and previous jobs and reasons for leaving; Education and training; Referees.

Describe why you are attracted to this job : relate your experience and skills to the requirements listed above.

2 UNIVERSITY LECTURER/SENIOR LECTURER IN COUNSELLING (0.7)
Main Duties/Responsibilities
Contribute to the teaching offered in Counselling and Psychotherapy including skills modules within a range of occupational training courses in addition to the Section's programme of Foundation Certificate (level 2), Postgraduate Diploma and Masters courses.

Contribute to the design, planning, and delivering of new courses: eg supervisor training.

Assessment and examination of students' work.

Engage in and support research activities.

Salary – up to £20,553 pa

Person Specification

Attributes	Essential	Desirable
Knowledge	Humanistic counselling theories. Applied person centred counselling. Social context, equal opportunities and oppression issues.	Person centred approach (central model). Other models/theories. Research methods.
Skills	Teaching/training counsellors. Assessing theoretical and practical work.	Research methods teaching.
Experience	Minimum of 5 years/1,000 hours of supervised counselling practice.	Research in counselling/therapy. Teaching at postgrad. level. Proven record as a teacher. One or more client specialisms.

Candidates invited for interview will be asked to give a 15 minute presentation on some aspect of their practice, research or teaching interests (selection criteria: clarity, structure and ability to hold the audience: present and future profile of interests and expertise). Candidates also participate in a 40 minute discussion on a training-related topic in the presence of members of the staff team (selection criteria: understanding of training issues: task and process skills in a group context).

Application Form

Personal details; Education and Qualifications; Membership of professional bodies; Training courses; Interests and achievements; Employment history; Referees.

Further information

Explain how your skills and experience are relevant to this position, and why you are applying. Include details of any research, consultancy and publications.

Case Study of an Established School Counsellor:- Patrina
Work Experience

Current:–

1989	School Counselling Service	Counsellor (to students, parents and staff)
1989	Private Practice	Counsellor
1990	Private Practice and Counselling Centre	Supervisor to Individuals and groups
1991	Social Services Supportline	Counsellor

1992	EAP	Counsellor
1995	College	Tutor on Counselling Certificate Course
1994	University	Co-Facilitator/Tutor for Interviewing Skills on Social Work Course
1993	University	Senior Counsellor (students and staff)

Previous:-

1992-93	Women's Refuge	Counsellor and Group Facilitator
1992-93	College	Lecturer in Social Care
1991-93	Adult Studies Centre	Tutor in Assertiveness Training, Personal Effectiveness and Stress Management
1990-92	Social Services	Independent Family Crisis Counsellor
1980-81	Local Authority	Social Worker
1976-80	Community Crisis Counselling Centre	Youth and Family Counsellor
1974-76	Student Social Worker	
1972-74	University	Secretary/Receptionist
	Local Authority	Counsellor for Adolescents on Probation
1969-70	Psychiatric Hospital	Social-Diversional Therapist

Education and Qualifications

1978	University	MSc in Social Work
1971	University	BA in Humanistic Psychology

Member of British Association for Counselling, Adlerian Society of Great Britain, Ericsonian Society of Great Britain, and Catalyst (a local association for counsellors and therapists).

The Job (school counsellor)

Usually five hours per week at girls grammar school (and four other schools) at £16.50 ph: flexibility with no waiting list: includes teachers, parents and friends when appropriate.

Selection Process

Interviewed by Consultant Paediatrician for the Health Authority who fund the service. New school counsellors are now interviewed by the Director and another team member. Understanding of the school system and the pressures on teachers is crucial in this job.

Counselling Training

Originally not all members of the counselling team were required to have a counselling diploma but now they do.

Household Context

Married with two dependent children: dual careers equally supported and home responsibilities shared.

Satisfactions

Working with young people who are open to learning new ways of managing their lives: the combination of self employment and being part of a supportive team: multi-disciplinary approach with a variety of clients: other inputs to school such as staff support and training peer counsellors: helping to empower people of any age.

Disappointments

When unable to help a client or find a suitable referral: eg a girl too angry to use support and parents themselves too angry and stressed to work on relationships.

Surprises

Often surprised and delighted when able to manage one of the school counsellors' worst scenarios, the angry parent: surprised when parents, upset to learn that their child was seeing a counsellor, agree to cooperate: surprised by how open many parents are to learning new ways of parenting and by people's strength through very difficult times.

Lucky Breaks

Getting interviewed for school counselling work at a time when there were very few counselling jobs: lucky to have had previous school experience and being in the right place at the right time: continue to be lucky in having such a good supervisor.

The Future

The school counselling service is growing, from four counsellors in 1990 to 11 in 1995 and the director plans to delegate some of the supervision: also develop a counselling diploma course, to follow on from the certificate, which will include some input on school counselling.

Advice for Budding School Counsellors

Get trained, especially a diploma. Contact the Counselling in Education Division (of BAC) for support and information. Find out what is happening locally by networking with counsellors, teachers and social work professionals. Approach your education or health authority about school counselling and funding: consider offering one term at no charge to schools as a taster. Be clear about what you can and cannot offer and on what terms.

Comment

Here is an interesting example of a 'portfolio' career with no fewer than six different sources of recent counselling income. Patrina has attended 59 training workshops or courses over a period of 15 years, has joined three existing professional associations and helped to create a fourth. This may well be a case of someone creating their luck. The combination of teaching, supervising, paid employment and private practice seems to work very well and it is no surprise that Patrina is hoping to set up a more advanced counselling course.

Case Study of an Established Counsellor:- Jonathan (early 50s)

Work Experience

1971	Lecturer/counsellor	College of FE.
1976-80	Open University Tutor (pt).	
1966-67	Schoolteacher.	

Education and Qualifications

1994	University	Cert. in Counselling
1987	Polytechnic	Diploma in Prof. Studies in Education (computing).
1974	University	D Phil. in English Literature.
1966	University	MA in English Literature

The Job
50% lecturer and 50% student counsellor at a college of further education, paid on an academic pay scale. In practice this means 11 hours of actual counselling over 36 weeks, and some more for another six weeks.

Selection Procedure
Asked to join the counselling team after working for a few years as a volunteer. No new counsellor would be appointed in this way and none has since. Now it is a full range of application letters, shortlists, interviews and case studies presented at interview.

Counselling Training
1994-5 Two year part-time Certificate in Counselling (University), £900 per term paid by employer. Entitles admission to Diploma which is expected to earn BAC accreditation. From 1971 Counselling Skills (short course) and a few since.

Household Context
Divorced with two grown up children.

Satisfactions
The best feature is playing a part in people's recovery from pain, loss, abuse and all the complicating difficulties of life. To be with people as they heal and recover, grow more self-accepting, find new energy and direction, is a privilege. Recent appointment of financial counsellor has taken away some unfavoured work, heavy at start of academic year.

Disappointments
Until recently the counselling service has not been effectively promoted within the college and there are certainly more people who could be helped.

Surprises
The range of ages and problems in the early years of counselling.

Lucky Breaks
Being asked to do the job all these years ago.

The future
Additional counsellors will be volunteers in order to save money. I anticipate more and more sense of fulfillment in counselling as I integrate my training and experience.

Advice to Budding Counsellors in Further Education
Obtain a certificate and preferably a diploma in counselling. Having experience of working in FE in another role and/or study at an FE college will help a lot.

Comment
Some counsellors in the 60s and 70s had the opportunity to start this work on the strength of their personality and voluntary work and this reflects the principle of amateurism in both teaching and support work in British further and higher education which prevailed at the time. However it's never too late to engage in high quality training and people like Jonathan bring a wealth of experience to their courses which enriches the work of all students of counselling.

Case Study of a High Flyer:– Sean
Education

1989	Open Business School	The Effective Manager (Diploma Module)
1971	University	Diploma in Applied Social Work
1969	University	BA Hons. in Modern History

Membership of Professional Bodies
Association of Student Counsellors; BAC.

Work Experience

1989	University	Director of Student Services.
1986-89	College of HE	Co-ordinator of Student Services
1978-86	Nat. IHE	Student Counsellor
1977-78	Private Practice	Family Caseworker
1975-77	Health Board	" "
1974-75	TV Company	Researcher
1973-74	Soc. Studies Institute	Researcher
1971-73	Local Authority	Probation Officer

The Job
Director of Student Services at a large northern university, including Counselling and Advisory Services, Accommodation, Chaplaincy, Student Health. Salary £34,000pa.

Selection Procedure
Informal session with section heads (45 mins.) and tour of facilities, followed by formal four person panel interview (also 45 mins.) The word 'informal' is very misleading because the current staff had ample opportunity to have their say which was subsequently taken into account.

Household Context
Married with one teenage daughter. My wife has a career in a caring profession but does not mind my career taking precedence over hers.

Satisfactions
Being able to deal with macro issues including preventative and developmental work: being part of a broader team, cutting across boundaries, for example with the registry over admissions and finance over student debt. Regular working hours.

Disappointments
People wanting to hang on to outdated boundaries: uncertainty of funding: uncertainty that the department can respond to challenges because of the weight of routine work. Much of my time is taken up with serious financial issues in student halls of residence which is a major distraction.

Surprises
That predictions have largely come true, partly explained by my knowledge of trends in North American universities.

Lucky Breaks
A friend working as a lecturer in psychology suggested that I might like to apply for a part-time counselling post at the local university. The workload increased rapidly and I was offered a full-time contract.

The Future

I enjoy my work and it may well be the case that further promotion, with or without a move is inappropriate. I have a well developed network of contacts and this results in advanced warning of vacancies such as dean of students and pro-vice chancellor.

Advice to Budding Directors of Student Services

Be alert to trends and the opportunities to gain experience in those trends. This is not always necessarily in higher education because in some respects innovation and reform has happened more quickly in further education. Look beyond counselling and aim to work across boundaries. Be alert and aware of organisational politics, especially the growing flexibility and fluidity which results in increasing emphasis on project teams, task forces and so on.

Comment

The reasons why Sean was successful included his energy, enthusiasm and commitment to growth and change. His vision was to see counselling within the wider context of the development of a range of support services which, wherever possible, would be integrated in the curriculum. Although he has been extremely successful in expanding and developing student services this has not happened through empire-building. His way is to work in partnership rather than in competition with academics and other staff.

Conclusions

Central government will surely come under increasing pressure to invest more heavily in high quality training and education, although at the time of writing (late 1996) the priorities appear to be the youngest age groups. Further and higher education are moving from a model of teaching knowledge to one of enabling learning, and employers are clamouring for that system to produce more self reliant students. These students should be aware of the the changing world of work, take responsibility for their own career and personal development, and be able to manage throughout life the relationships with work and with learning . All this should include an enhanced role for student and adult guidance and support systems, and therefore hopefully more jobs.

I find it difficult to envisage counselling, with its focus on deeply seated problems requiring slow and lengthy treatment, surviving in this traditional form. This is not intended as a criticism but a forecast that further and higher education colleges will opt for a counselling, guidance and advisory service that is short-term focussed and woven into the fabric of new forms of teaching and pastoral care. Some of this will actually be accommodated within the curriculum, further eroding the distinction between teaching and non-teaching functions. BAC accreditation will be desirable for counselling staff and within the team will be other people such as reception staff trained to NVQ levels 2 and 3. I think this is an attractive scenario.

CHAPTER 6:
COUNSELLING IN PASTORAL CARE SETTINGS

Introduction

"There are more trainee counsellors than Church of England Clerics" . . . says Lesley White (1997) in her lively and readable review of the UK counselling industry.

The complexity of the counselling scene is a recurring theme of this book and it is this characteristic which Lyall (1995) emphasises at the very start of his excellent book 'Counselling in the Pastoral and Spiritual Setting'. He points out that there is now much more diversity in the Church, both lay and ordained, and many men and women regard themselves as offering a counselling ministry. Some will call themselves pastoral counsellors who are in practice heavily dependent on secular therapies, but others, of the conservative evangelical strand, see themselves as more avowedly Christian counsellors basing their approach upon what they believe to be Biblical truth. The latter will make more explicit use of Biblical language and ideas in the counselling process and they will tend to be more ambivalent towards the the insights of psychology. The uniqueness of counselling in this context is, arguably, that the roots of the modern counselling movement are themselves deeply embedded in the traditions of the Church's ministry of pastoral care.

Whilst regular church attenders are in a tiny minority most people believe in some kind of God or have some sense of a spiritual dimension to their being. This suggests to me that counselling may present an excellent opportunity to help people explore their most fundamental values and perhaps re-invent themselves spiritually. This certainly has more appeal for me, a sceptical methodist, than the idea that I am engaged with my client primarily in an exercise in behaviour modification for straightforward rational purposes. Lyall (1995) surmises that it is not entirely accidental that the emergence of a more pluralistic society and the disappearance of some commonly held stories, beliefs and values has been accompanied by the growth of the counselling movement.

"In an age when shared stories seem to be losing their potency, it becomes more important than ever that people should make sense of their own personal stories." (Lyall; 135)

However, it would be quite wrong to think that the influence of particular beliefs or values are unique to pastoral counselling. The idea of value free counselling is a myth and there is no context in which the beliefs and values of counsellors and their clients do not impinge in some way on their relationship. We now live in an increasingly pluralistic society and it is important to acknowledge that, for example, whereas western psychotherapies assert their independence in relation to the world, eastern psychologies may require the renunciation of individuality. Of course, the greater the distance in terms of values and beliefs between counsellor and client the harder it is to counsel effectively. This was one of the main reasons for setting up the Race division of the BAC.

"the greater the distance in culture and beliefs"

Lyall (1995) notes the expansion in recent years of the role of ministers, not just Christian, in industry, hospitals, prisons and so on. His personal experience as hospital chaplain was that counselling relationships of some depth could develop, and there were numerous counselling opportunities with the relatives of patients and also hospital staff. The Association of Christian Counsellors was established to ensure that these counsellors work to professional standards recognized by secular organisations.

From Freud and Jung to Rogers

Lyall (1995: 9) examines the early psychoanalytic influence of Freud and Jung.

"Jung could not accept Freud's reductionism, his belief that all human behaviour could be explained in terms of instinctive drives, nor his insistence that the roots of all pathology were sexual. Similarly, Freud was troubled by Jung's positive evaluation of the place of religion in human life."

Not surprisingly Jung's theories of personality are more acceptable to some Christians.

Carl Rogers, the guru of person centred counselling, has clearly been very important in the growth of pastoral counselling as an autonomous professional discipline. Certain characteristics of the ideal helping relationship have almost become normative for all types of counselling: genuineness, non-possessive warmth and accurate empathy. Person centred counselling/psychotherapy has been regarded as a relatively safe method especially for a counsellor of limited training, and Rogers was popular with the religious liberals because they liked his optimistic image of the self as capable of growth and change. I recall how as a person-centred counselling trainee I keenly embraced the notion of Man's intrinsic goodness but I have become more sceptical in my later years. Interestingly Rogers' last book, 'A Way of Being' (1980), was much more aware of the transcendentent and mystical dimension of human life.

The subsequent growth of a wide range of psychotherapies such as Transactional Analysis and Gestalt Therapy inevitably led to a loosening of connection with the traditional modes of Christian ministry whilst affirming the integrity of these secular approaches. Lyall (1995) wonders whether some new kind of integration is possible: having recently resumed my churchgoing following a serious illness I would like to think so.

In the 1970s the Association for Pastoral Care and Counselling was one of three organisations that set up the British Association for Counselling (BAC). Meanwhile within the Churches themselves professionalism in pastoral care began to be taken more seriously, such as in hospitals and universities, but sometimes it is difficult to establish the precise boundaries of professional competence and concern. For example, when I started student counselling in 1981 I was surprised to discover that there was no clear consensus about the range of student problems that the college chaplain was 'qualified' to deal with. I had assumed that a minister was automatically qualified to deal with the full range of people's concerns, a piece of baggage I had no doubt brought with me from my methodist upbringing. Later I was to learn that, regardless of your beliefs, precise training and experience, it is vital that you know when to refer clients to appropriate other experts. In the USA ordination is a prerequisite for accreditation as a pastoral counsellor and so 'lay' pastoral care cannot be 'professional'. In Britain, where Betjamin famously described all professions as 'conspiracies against the laity', pastoral counsellors can be both lay and professional.

Two Types of Caring

Lyall (1995) sees two ministries, with the emergence of a separate breed of specially trained pastoral counsellors, as a comparatively recent phenomenon:-

Pastoral Care	Counselling
Pastor makes the first approach	Parishioner takes the initiative
Implicit contract	Explicit negotiated contract
Hesitant over resistance	Open about resistance
Aware of transference and counter-transference	More skilled in transference and counter-transference

What begins as pastoral care, which has its own integrity, may soon develop into a counselling relationship (Could we meet to talk about this at greater length?) and then the pastor needs to be aware of the changed dynamics of the relationship.

One of the distinctive strengths of pastoral counselling is that it takes place within the wider context of pastoral care with the potential support of a caring community. I acknowledge that whether or not people come asking for counselling, ministers must have counselling skills in order to respond effectively. The Westminster Pastoral Foundation has been a major contributor to the promotion of counselling in the pastoral/spiritual context, with their network of some 50 counselling centres spread around Britain. These centres offer both training and counselling and the trainees are predominantly both lay and women: some will be quite agnostic in their religious views but enrol in the courses because the training is good. Clients are self-referred or may be referred by others such as ministers, either because the relevant skills are not available locally or because there are advantages for the client being given help within the relative anonymity of the counselling centre. I recall when a close friend was suffering from depression he was very reluctant to approach his minister. This was partly because he was a lapsed presbyterian and he dreaded the thought that the minister might want them to pray together. He was uncertain about the minister's training and qualifications and my friend certainly preferred the relative anonymity of a separate, professional counselling service.

Lyall identifies three ways in which religion can have therapeutic potential:–
    i   The universality of human religious experience.
    ii   Religious experience can be an aid to diagnosis. The spiritual journey of the client is nearly always a reflection of important themes in that person's life.
    iii   The therapeutic potential of religious resources. Counsellors working in a secular arena may underestimate the significance of a religious faith in the lives of their clients.

Issues
Krebs (1980) lists four problems which are inherent to the practice of counselling in parish ministry:–
    i   The promise of cheap growth. Parishioners will often be looking for a quick and painless solution to their problems.
    ii   Transference. The pastor cannot assume the role of anonymous, faceless analyst.
    iii   Role confusion. Combining the role of therapist with many other diverse roles including teacher, committee member etc. Confidentiality becomes impossible.
    iv   Misplaced priorities. Long-term counselling distracts from many other tasks.

Switzer (1983) challenges these points by stressing the scope for brief counselling (6-8 sessions), the ability to recognize transference when it takes place, and the fact that role confusion is simply a fact of parish life. However, there is no tradition among the clergy that they should undergo counselling training as part of their preparation for the intense pastoral work that most of them undertake. Today there is a widespread awareness of the reality of stress in parochial ministry and the fact is that the clergy are no different from other helping professions in their need for support and high quality supervision. Throughout the caring professions there is widespread concern about the phenomenon of 'burnout' and the clergy are no exception. Research by Irvine (1989) indicated that isolation was evident in three primary areas:–
    i   Professional isolation: a lack of support from colleague and other professionals.
    ii   Social isolation: meeting other people solely as 'the minister'.
    iii   Spiritual isolation; lacking others who would minister to them.

I also recall advice that was given in good faith to a friend of mine soon after he was ordained at 35 and still single. When visiting lonely single women of 'a certain age' he was advised by a retired vicar to 'keep your coat on and sit near the door!'
    There are in private practice a number who profess a spiritual component in their counselling model and in counselling centres set up by church bodies much of

"Don't take your coat off and sit by the door"

the work is done by lay volunteers. The extent to which counsellors in pastoral care settings can enjoy fruitful co-operation with other professionals depends upon the extent to which they are perceived by others, and themselves, as 'professional' in the best sense of the word. Lyall (1995) notes that sometimes social activists accuse counsellors of a 'psychological quietism' which tries to help people adjust to their problems while turning a blind eye to the social and political roots of these problems. A recent secular example of this was when a counsellor offered to set up a stress management group in her institution. This outraged some trade union representatives who highlighted the need for action by the unions to eliminate the sources of stress themselves.

A Morning with Paul – a Baptist Minister

Setting the scene: I see Brian and Peter separately on Tuesday mornings each week. They are both ministers of religion (as I am), and so much of our talk is about the work of the ministry and of the Church. The two relationships differ a little from one another. I have been meeting with Brian for fifteen years, and we use the hour and a half we are together for mutual support which ebbs and flows according to personal circumstances. Sometimes I am the one doing the off-loading, at other times it is Brian. With Peter the situation is much more that I am his counsellor and spiritual director. With Brian, therefore meetings tend to be much more unstructured with very little directive input from either of us. In Peter's case, he wants me to stand not simply as a sympathetic listener, but as a guide into a spirituality which will support and strengthen him. Both Brian and Peter suffer from depression. In Brian's case this arises from his disenchantment with the structure of the Church in which he is a senior member of the regional organisation, and his loneliness as a widower with no children. In Peter's case the depression springs from feelings of inadequacy as a working-class man in a predominantly middle-class calling, where his ways of thinking and operating are not those of the majority of his colleagues, or indeed of his congregation.

One morning I visit Brian at quarter to nine. I am a little late – usually I arrive at about twenty past eight. This morning has begun badly for me with a letter in my post which has left me feeling angry and frustrated by its style and contents. In a particularly busy period just before Easter, when I am myself psychologically tired, I fail to leave home at my usual time because my emotions blind me to the simple tasks of finding my diary and my building society passbook. I calm down in the drive to Brian's house, but need to finish letting off steam. In his kitchen as he makes our ritual cup of coffee, Brian lets me tell him how I am. "How are you?" is a genuine question between us, and we are allowed to answer honestly.

My little storm blows itself out – in a coffee cup rather than a tea cup – as Brian begins to tell me of a woman whose son in South Africa she was recently visiting. With her son and daughter-in-law she was mugged. Since they had no money she and her pregnant daughter-in-law were beaten up, taken away in a lorry and dumped, while her son was shot in the back of the head. She has returned to her home in the Midlands, and phones Brian for his help. As the story emerges, I ask myself what would I have done, how I would have listened, what I would have said. The tragedy is appalling, and like Brian, I feel that all we can offer in such situations is ourselves. Brian is exhausted from the encounter which kept him out till very late. In this counselling situation, there is no advice to give. The task is simply to review what has occurred and to affirm Brian in his skill as a listener and minister.

Much of pastoral ministry is humdrum, and many ministers suggest that they are good in a crisis. By this they often mean that they are able to offer strategies and advice to those in distress. Brain is less assertive; yet I judge that his willingness to drop everything for someone outside his pastoral care and sit for hours quietly listening shows a degree of crisis management which will lead eventually to a positive outcome. For him the crisis had begun with a woman howling in pain on the telephone; when she left she was still in pain, but she was less frightened and had a greater belief that she would cope – even with the possibility of returning to South Africa as witness should the criminals ever be brought to court. Brian's story left me once more realising that in counselling the counsellor learns as much – if not more – than the counselled. I am constantly amazed by the resources of human beings in the very deepest traumas. We are far more resilient than we imagine, and very often what we need is some one to restore our elasticity.

My visit to Peter is more structured, not least since he asked me to be his spiritual director nearly a year ago when he was emerging from a very severe clinical depression. Again we begin with coffee – to be a counsellor you must either have a strong bladder or easy access to a loo! Peter has suffered the disappointment of not getting a job for which he was short-listed and eminently well qualified. His only teenage daughter has just had an abortion, and he feels guilty about supporting her in that decision (should he approve of abortion?) and with his wife and daughter he feels great pain in the agony of the last few days. The congregation he serves is elderly and reluctant to change. They demand of him skills he does not possess, but do not support and foster the gifts he does have. He finds ministry psychologically and emotionally draining and even damaging.

In my role as spiritual director, I am not there simply to to give him a sympathetic hearing and to review various possibilities in a manner detached from my own emotional and spiritual commitment to him. As he tells me the events of the previous fortnight he is clearly in intense pain. I take my shoes off as a signal to him that I am going to tread on holy ground. We begin to talk about how his spiritual trauma and his emotional exhaustion feed one another and forebode a dark night of the soul. I encourage him to write a spiritual diary in this Holy Week and to read in the remaining days of the Gospel accounts in turn of the Passion. I encourage him to keep his descriptive material free from analysis and comment, and only to begin any thinking after he has recorded his feelings. We talk about the person he is as a person called by God to ministry. We talk about his wounds being part of what he must offer first to God and then to the world.

Peter is a very special minister; he suffers an emotional "bleeding" in all he does. Although he longs to love people, his rawness makes the cost very high. At times his love turns to hatred, and this is such a time. Peter's church tradition is very success-oriented, and he feels a failure. To me he is an icon of Christ. I tell him so, and when I leave I hug him in the doorway. If the neighbours are watching what the hell? Peter is in a desert and he needs a guide who will give him a path through the trackless sands. I drive away having learned far more than I could teach. Once again, I have witnessed heroic determination to persist in the face of great psychic pain. In this part of my life I am nourished by the fortitude of those who count themselves weak.

Training

There is simply no room in normal Bachelor of Divinity courses for the required degree of specialization in counselling. A sample of training courses currently available in the UK are:–

1. **Introductory Level** (BAC-1 star):–
    i   St. George's Hospital, London. Part-time courses in Pastoral Care.
    ii   Devon Pastoral Counsellors Totnes. Foundation Course in Counselling: 1 year part-time.
    iii Bethlehem Royal & Maudsley Special Health Authority. Pastoral Care: part-time.

2. **Advanced Level** (BAC-2 star):–
    i   Clinical Theology Association, Oxford. Pastoral Counselling & Pastoral Care: 2 years part-time and an advanced year.
    ii   St. George's Hospital, London. Pastoral Education: Full-time.
    iii Westminster Pastoral Foundation, London and elsewhere in UK. The situation of their advanced courses is ambiguous in that the are listed in the BAC Training Directory as 'pastoral care' but this is not clear from the course descriptions.
    iv   Devon Pastoral Counsellors, Totnes. Advanced Tng in Counselling: 2 years part-time.
    v   Bethlehem Royal & Maudsley Special Health Authority. Pastoral Edn: 11 weeks full time.

vi Birmingham University. MA/Diploma in Pastoral Studies: 1 year full time or 2
     years part time.
(Source: BAC Training Directory 1996)

The advent of National Vocational Qualifications (NVQs) may be very significant,
with a shift of emphasis from knowledge to competence that many will welcome.
But Lyall (1995) wonders whether methods of assessment based on so-called
performance criteria might miss the deeper nuances of human interaction and the
complex dimensions of the human spirit.

Typical Jobs
1 PROJECT MANAGER (Christian Fellowship)
Job Description
1   To make proposals for the retention, variation and development of high
       standard childcare policies and their implementation, and evaluate their
       effectiveness
2   To provide a care plan for each young person and safeguard their welfare.
3   To be responsible for the induction and supervision of staff.
4   To be responsible for the recruitment, deployment of domestic staff.
5   To manage financial arrangements.
6   To establish arrangements for the collection of contributions, allocation of
       funds, and applications for appropriate benefits.

Person Specification
Social Work Qualification,
Minimum 3 years client group experience,
Staff supervision experience,
Position of seniority,
Knowledge of child development, social policy as it effects young people leaving
care, Children's Care Act 1989,
Presentation and inter-personal skills,
Understanding of budget and management issues in residential care.
Salary £19,830-£21,423 pa.

Application Form
Personal Details incl. Health, References, Education/Qualifications, Relevant Training/
Membership of Professional Bodies, Leisure Pursuits/ Hobbies, Voluntary Social Work,
Current and Past Employment
Any Other Information/Why Seeking This Post?

2 PROJECT WORKER (Therapeutic Community)
Job Description
1   Contributing and assisting in therapeutic programme development, maintenance
       and review.
2   Assisting in selection, induction and supervision of volunteers.
3   Assist director with records, compliance with client contracts, health and
       safety legislation and building maintenance.

4   Liaison with other agencies, and develop links with local community.
5   Participate in training
6   Participate in chapel services.
7   Promote equal opportunities.

Application Form

Personal Details, Career History, Leisure Interests, Positions of Responsibility (non-work), References, **Why are you applying /additional information in support, Which job have you enjoyed most? What would you enjoy most about this position? Please summarise in one sentence your religious beliefs.**

Case Study of a Pastoral Care Tutor/Private Practitioner. Fiona (forties)
Work Experience.
Ongoing

1995-   Head of Counselling, Pastoral Counselling Service.
1993-   Lecturer (part-time) in Pastoral Psychology (LPP), Theological College.
1991-   Local Supervisor/ Growth Work Tutor for Dip. in Pastoral Counselling
(college)

Also

1992-94 Intake Worker and Committee Member (Pastoral Counselling Service).
1989-92 Voluntary Counsellor (Charity).
1976-92 Small Business (with husband: many varied tasks including marketing, administration, managing, recruiting, teaching computing and publications: several years full-time and subsequently part-time).
1976-77 Social Work Assistant (rehabilitation centre).
1974-76 Canada: 18 months as Housemother/Music Teacher, 6 months as Nursing Assistant (old people's home).
1973-74 Social Work Assistant (hospital).

Other Teaching

Myers-Briggs workshops, gender and sexuality course unit (for mental health charity, CFE).

Education & Qualifications

1993   MSc. in Psychological Counselling (university).
1991   Dip. in Psychological Counselling (university).
1973   MA Philosophy and Psychology (university).

Therapy

5 Years in Analysis: 6 months in Counselling.
Total costs of training/therapy approx. £16,000.

The Jobs

1   Head of Counselling (PCS): Honorarium (£100-£500 pa).
2   Private Practice: 20 hours pw: sliding scale £10-£25 ph (at home).
3   Tutor (LPP): 1 day pw (term-time): £15 ph.

Selection Procedure

1   By invitation of counselling team.
2   By clients! (word of mouth).
3   Interview.

Household Context
Husband and one dependent child.

Satisfactions
People (always interesting), freedom of operation, no commuting, seeing change take place.

Disappointments
Lack of institutional support, work space intrusion on family space, spending much time contemplating the limits of experience.

Surprises
Being readily accepted on the scene.

Lucky Breaks
Being able to move across gradually from business without financial hardship: Good friends.

The Future
To continue as I am, learning all the time. To consolidate PCS. To get off the ground a public forum to discuss issues around psychoanalysis and religion.

Advice to Budding Pastoral Care/Private Practitioners
Be sure that you want to do this: network: take your own therapy very seriously: know what your supports and resources are.

Comment
This is an interesting 'portfolio' existence, with income, albeit sometimes in modest quantities, coming from as many as seven different sources over a period of time. Bearing in mind the high cost of training/therapy it was obviously helpful to fit her career change and development around her husband's successful business. Fiona is a very versatile woman and seems now to be well established and reasonably secure in an insecure world.

Case Study of a High Flyer – James (47)
Work Experience

1995	Christian Counselling Institute Director (CCI).
	Private Practice (10 hours pw.) Tutor/Counsellor (Open Univ.)
	Mental Health Employment Project (MHEP) (Voluntary).
1991-93	Head of Counselling (CCI).
1991-93	Coordinator (MHEP).
1986-89	Lay Pastor. Tutor/Counsellor (OU).
1985-86	Tutor (A-level College). Wrote Travel Book.
1980-85	Teacher (Zimbabwe).
1975-80	OU Tutor and Staff Tutor. Teacher of Complementary Studies (Art College, as in 'Wilt' by Tom Sharpe!).
1971-80	Smallholding.

Education

1992-94	MA Counselling.
1990-91	Intro Course, Institute of Group Analysis.
1989-90	Diploma in Counselling (placement in Polytechnic) .

1987-90 Co-counselling.

1967-70 BA in Economics and Art History.

1991-95 Personal Therapy – 4 years, initially twice per week and then 3 times.

The Job

Director of Christian Counselling Institute (CCI): £13,000 pa pro-rata: approx. 25 hours pw): accommodation limited in space and time.

Selection Procedure (CCI)

Initial interview: negotiated job description.

Household Context

Married 24 years. Wife earns similar salary: important because earned very little 1989-92.

Satisfactions

i   CCI. Relations to colleagues: exciting philosophical underpinning: growing reputation of national agency (invited to lead workshops etc).

ii   Private Practice. Deep mutual understanding from working with one client twice per week over 3/4 years: Rawness/nakedness of challenge of clients (incl. non-Christians) straight off the street: Proper pay recorded in accounts book.

Disappointments

i   CCI. Some good individuals but management lacks commitment and understanding of the work : poor pay (take home £570 pm).

ii   Private Practice. Many at first, fewer now: people leaving prematurely.

Surprises

The contradictory mix of the evangelicals: for example homophobia in people with many qualities: they rail against cults but that is what they are.

Lucky Breaks

Taken on by brilliant supervisor (career midwife): previous director of CCI left after only nine months.

The Future

Postgraduate training in Integrative Body Psychotherapy: involved in new project for counselling/healing centre (£500,000 to go) – possible new home for greatly expanded CCI (from 4 to 17 rooms: from cosy middle-class suburb to tough, working class area): when youngest child reaches college, free to live elsewhere (open space, sea, animals?).

Advice to Budding CCI Directors

Much good can come from the evangelical/fundamentalist church such as growth and change including counselling. Their Association of Christian Counsellors will work towards a national system of training and supervision which is to be welcomed. But there remains a residue of deep suspicion: for example they will refuse to affiliate to the BAC. There is much inconsistency: for example one prominent local evangelical church recently suspended counselling because it "gets in the way of God's will". Beware the 'bible-bashers' and the most ghastly forms of Christian Imperialism. There is a market niche for an intelligent, moderate, integrative approach, and the work will include helping victims to work through the follies of extreme evangelism. Get good supervision and avoid isolation: if there is no contact or support group of counsellors in your area then start one up. Try out different settings as they are very different from each other and this will deepen your understanding of the context for counselling. Strike a balance between counselling and other proactive or creative activities, and if you work psychodynamically, then no more than 15 clients per week: in other words counsel part-time! " Every therapist should have a garden"

Conclusions

The pastoral care setting is where the mystery of counselling interacts with the deeper mystery of spirituality and religion, sometimes generating conflict rather than consensus. But for both counsellor and client the power of faith is likely to play a major part in the healing process. Of all the varied settings for counselling this may be the one that pre-dates psychology and within which it is particularly important that counsellor and client are well matched in their belief systems. If you prefer to see human issues in terms of black and white then counselling is not for you: it's the shades of grey that make it fascinating, to say nothing of the occasional shafts of light.

CHAPTER 7:
COUNSELLING IN THE COMMUNITY

Introduction

The practice of counselling is not as neatly and tidily arranged as the chapter headings of this book seem to suggest and this is particularly true of the community setting. Local churches, general practices, local authorities, charities and other independent organisations can all be said to play their part in providing counselling and related services in the 'community' and it by no means unusual for two or more agencies to work in partnership and also share premises. That richness and diversity is reflected in the fact that many counsellors work in more than one of these settings, with the record being held by Megan (see chapter on private practice) who works in six different settings including the community.

For this book I am interpreting community as including charities, local authority social services, independent counselling centres and special projects. The main concerns in counselling in the community include relationships, substance misuse, sexually transmitted diseases, criminal behaviour, homelessness, mental illness and bereavement, with the more obvious overlaps being with medical settings. The work is often directed at particular vulnerable groups such as ethnic minorities, young people, single parents and victims of crime, and much of this work is done by trained volunteers who are supervised and led by full and part-time professional staff. Many of the counsellors are members of the Personal/Sexual/Marital/Family Division which is the largest in the BAC. In order to give an insight into counselling in the community I have examined eight recently advertised jobs in eight different types of agency and, as in other settings, I analyse two further jobs in detail and report three case studies of practitioners.

Young People

One typical charity based in a big city deals with the 16 to 25 age group and 80% of their clients indicate depression as an issue, with the rising suicide rate for young men

"depression – a growing issue for young people"

being a particular cause for concern. At their 1993 AGM a Director of a National Youth Agency estimated that more than 100,000 young people between 16 and 25 are not 'accounted for', i.e. they are not employed, on youth training schemes, courses, or claiming benefit. New funding from a city Family Health Service and the local authority will enable this charity to expand and reduce their six week waiting list. During 1994 the service provided 1261 individual counselling sessions, 113 initial interviews, 784 telephone sessions and 14 other enquiries. 65% of clients were female and more than half were self referred. 41% were in work, 33% unemployed, 18% students and 8% at school. A significant increase in Asian clients was noted from 3% in 1993 to 15% in 1994.

Specialist counselling is available in some areas for children and young people who have been sexually abused and the non-abusing parent. One scheme is a collaborative venture between a children's charity and a local authority. The therapeutic approach will be concerned with establishing a safe place in which survivors might challenge the negative view which they usually have of themselves in consequence of the violence, intimidation and betrayal perpetrated by the abuser. A social work qualification is likely to be needed for work of this nature, plus knowledge and experience of child abuse.

A Multicultural Society

Give the multi-cultural nature of our society some jobs will require applicants to have the appropriate cultural background and perhaps be fluent in two or more languages. An Asian organisation recently recruited a project worker to help Asian women with mental problems. Although no particular qualifications were essential applicants must have knowledge and experience in mental health and community work, and good counselling and interpersonal skills. A distinctive feature of this job was the importance of being able to advocate on behalf of Asian women their needs and requirements within the mental health system, and to raise general awareness of these needs.

Another example of working with black people is a project jointly set up between a charity and local authority to help black care leavers. This is a group project whose main focus is to empower black young people in coping with discrimination and racism within society. These black young people are thought to learn a negative view of black culture through the media and as a result develop poor self esteem. Sessional workers for these clients do not necessarily have to have relevant qualifications but they do have to have proven experience of working with black young people and substantial experience of social groupwork.

Counsellors can specialise in working with offenders and in some jobs experience of a particular ethnic group is an advantage. One local authority has set up a Community Penalties Team to work with sexual offenders aged 15 to 17, particularly black young people. A relevant qualification would normally be required such as in social work, counselling, or educational psychology. Essential experience includes working with African, Caribbean and white offending young people in multi-cultural inner city areas. Not surprisingly active commitment to challenging racism and sexism in the workplace and the criminal justice system is essential and applicants will be eliminated if they fail to display adequate knowledge and commitment to the principles of equal opportunity.

Drugs, Alcohol and HIV

Support services for drug users and related illness are either available as part of the NHS or from independent organisations or a combination of the two. One fairly typical independent service is open to anyone concerned about their own drug use or that of another person. It will see people who are using a variety of substances from cannabis to heroin, and people using the service do not have to be drug free. The scheme does not try to make people stop using drugs but will support people who want to stop and also those who want help with the problems caused by drug use. Counselling and advice is offered to enable people to become stable, to reduce damage caused by drugs and to become drug free, by individual appointment, over the telephone, and some group work.

Assessment and referral to residential rehabilitation units, medical and other agencies is available. Also available are free needles, syringes, condoms and specialist advice on related health problems, plus practical help and advice on housing, the law, education, employment, welfare rights and so on. The scheme includes assessments and reports for people going through the court system and help with diversion from custody. It offers consultancy for social workers, community health and youth workers, probation officers, GPs and other agencies and persons in contact with drug users. Also offered are specifically designed training programmes.

The advisory/counselling service and drop in service was used by 242 individuals in 1993-4, of whom 225 were problem drug users. 1,400 hours were spent in counselling and over 8,000 hours of drop in time. For a job of drugs and HIV support worker a relevant qualification is essential, such as counselling, social work or nursing, plus training in HIV infection issues and counselling from a appropriate source. Also essential is experience of working with drug users and experience in person centred counselling.

In some areas a comprehensive residential facility is available for treating people addicted to drugs or alcohol. A trainee group worker would ideally have experience in the caring professions and/or completion of a treatment programme within alcohol/drug residential rehabilitation, an understanding of the issues involved in this work, and an understanding of clients' needs in a residential setting. Other essential requirements include commitment to equal opportunities, understanding of anti-discriminatory practice, communication skills, driving licence, plus abilities to work as part of a team, liaise with other professionals and establish appropriate personal and professional boundaries. For more senior positions management experience in a caring profession is essential, together with a relevant professional qualification.

Counselling Gay Men

In some parts of the country special projects have been set up for counselling gay men, especially to promote good health. One particular scheme in Scotland aims to work towards the prevention of the further transmission of HIV and to promote the health and well-being of gay men infected and affected by HIV/AIDS. This project is not designed as a 'quick fix' but rather a range of initiatives intended to deliver a mixture of short, medium and long term benefits, all with a view to 'normalising' the access and delivery of health and social care services to homosexual and bisexual people. Central to the health and well-being of gay men are the services of GPs but a needs assessment showed that access to and reception by GPs was of low quality. This was to be tackled by offering training, factsheets and guidelines, negotiating with primary care teams, and encouraging the formation of a broad grouping of GPs prepared to work in professional circles to improve services. There would also be collaborative work with other agencies such as Brook Advisory, and raising awareness of social workers.

Schools may be considered to be well served by the existing HIV and Sexual Health Team but the emphasis which can be put on gay sexuality is severely limited. Education is usually focused on heterosexual values and therefore gay teenagers will 'turn off' or feel devalued by this experience. Links can more easily be established in further and higher education with gay and lesbian societies, students unions and counselling services. In this scheme there is to be group work and one to one counselling, plus information and advice. Volunteers will be trained in administrative support, publicity, assisting the drop in facility and in group work.

A Day in the Life of Liam (57)

I work in an independent counselling service which operates out of the local community centre in our town. I deal with the full range of issues but have become very much a specialist in relationship work, partly because I trained originally with Relate (MGC then). Nearly all my clients are referred by current or previous clients and now I even have a short waiting list. This surprises me bearing in mind the struggle we had in the early days to set up the service and now I am delighted to be able to pass on some new clients to my two partners in whom I have enormous confidence. I insist on working strict part-time hours (12 per week maximum) because I do find the work emotionally draining and I like to balance it with my other job as a potter.

Daphne (49) has been seeing me off and on for nearly two years concerning her very troubled relationship with Simon. Her recurring question is "how can he treat me so badly"? to which a common sense reply would be "because he is like that". Of course sometimes Simon treats her well, taking her out to dinner for example, and their sex life certainly has its moments. On the other hand he takes little trouble to conceal the fact he sleeps with other women, for example at conferences which he frequently attends, and his bad behaviour extends to never remembering her birthday or buying her so much as a Christmas present. Daphne is on the brink of recognising that she would rather have this relationship that none at all.

Gwen has come on her own this time which is not unusual, with William her husband away again pursuing his hobby of fossil collecting. The pattern over the previous 18 months is for a furious row to erupt, with threats of separation and divorce etc. followed by reconciliation, declarations that 'this time we have talked everything through' and counselling is discontinued, until the next flare up. "Everything is fine" she declares with a smile and I breathe an inward sigh of relief as Gwen in full flow about "that man" is an impressive but wearing experience. She relates the tale of their most recent short break down at Brighton: they are both semi-retired and quite well off and seem to be forever going away on these 'activity breaks', this one being water colour painting. Perhaps it was the combination of the restful activity of painting, the fresh sea air and a bottle of wine with their evening meal, but apparently William came over all romantic for a change. Gwen never shows the slightest embarrassment talking about about her sex life, perhaps gauging accurately that I am shock proof in this area. She relates how they were in the middle of making love when immediately outside their sea-front bedroom window a brass band struck up, and she swears blind that William 'finished' as she put it when fireworks exploded nearby. We laugh, an all too rare experience for me with Gwen, so I enjoy it while I can. I nevertheless insist on steering the conversation back to the serious issue of their turbulent relationship which has been focussed on Gwen's perfectionism and failure to come to terms with William's retirement and tendency to doss around at home. This relationship will run and run I suspect and, who knows, may even run its full course.

Ben and Emma are a delightful but shy couple who came to see me for the first time last week in a state of acute embarrassment. Unusually for the 1990s both were virgins when they married four months ago and their love life had been a huge disappointment to the both of them. At the suggestion of their local vicar they had plucked up the courage and decided to seek counselling. My friend the minister knows that low key sex therapy is a speciality of mine. Last week I had quickly established that the main problem was premature ejaculation, very common in young men of course but Ben did not know this, never having talked about sex or even, astonishingly, read anything about it. I had been able to offer them some immediate reassurance and, as a previous sufferer myself in my early married life, I was able to use 'counsellor self disclosure' with confidence. I used to self disclose very sparingly but the more I counsel the more I find it seems to help. They are visibly more relaxed and even able to laugh a bit about last week's bedroom encounters. They had found the book I lent them very helpful and because I am able to talk to them in very straightforward language the 'taboo' subject of sex is dissolving before our very eyes. They are a delightful and loving couple and maybe one more session is all they will want or need.

Sarah (39), a hospital doctor, has not been to see me for about three months and surprises me by bringing along her new partner Brendon (late 40s). Sarah is another perfectionist whose long term boyfriend had, inevitably, enormous difficulty of living up to her high expectations. They eventually split up and it transpires Sarah had not so much come along for 'counselling' as wanting me to meet Brendon who by all accounts is the ideal partner. Should I charge my usual fee? I immediately warm to Brendon, a laid back professional musician and widower with a 14 year old daughter and it is obvious that he loves Sarah for her very considerable qualities, her wit, beauty and intelligence. He simply refuses to play along with her perfectionistic games and refuses even to give up smoking the occasional joint, but has agreed amicably to cut down still further. I find myself envying his pony-tail and wonder what my clients would think if I started to grow one! I am surprised to hear that already Sarah is planning to move into Bendon's rambling Edwardian house and I wonder about the ensuing family dynamics: Sarah has the capability to play 'wicked step-mother' and I tactfully suggest that the two of them arrange to see me after the move. "Why not" says Brendon as if I had invited them for a drink. Sarah looks at him adoringly. Has she finally met her match? I hope so.

My last client of the day fails to show but I hardly mind as it was one of my least favourites, an embittered divorcee who cannot let go his hatred for his ex-wife who left him for a younger man. This means an early trip to the golf course and time to fit in some practice before playing with my regular buddies. I hang out with an odd bunch, the one thing they all have in common is that they all took early retirement, never regretted it and as a result all lead more balanced and interesting lives. I am regarded as the group 'intellectual' and today I am able to explain to my friends that we apparently are now to be known as 'downshifters', people who *choose* to work and earn less and are much happier as a result. My remarks attract the customary ribaldry as we head off for the first tee of our very down-market golf course. With the benefit of my extra practice my first ball sails into the far distance, taking with it, as always, any lingering frustrations of my work as a counsellor. Golf for my buddies is less than therapeutic and the usual cursing ensues.

Typical Jobs
1 SENIOR PROJECT WORKER – Substance Abuse (Independent Charity)
Responsibilities
Therapeutic programme development, staff management and supervision, administration and finance, external contacts, funding and public relations, internal

contact and support, supervision and training, and equal opportunities. Salary £12,861 plus up to £1,000pa.

Person Specification

    i Essential

Minimum 1 year's experience of both relationship work and counselling and/or group work.

Knowledge and skills in communication, numeracy, equal opportunities, planning work, delegation, supervision and presentation. Self awareness, deal with stress, integrity and commitment to philosophy and objectives. Able to on-call and other anti-social hours, able to attend events and meetings and able to climb stairs.

    ii   Desirable:

Residential work experience, supervising/training, able to use Microsoft Works 2 or Wordperfect 5.1, knowledge of confidentiality, drug use, licence and tenancy agreements and registered homes legislation.

Application Form

Personal Details, References, Education and Training, Employment History, Health. **Outline your main interest in working for us and in this particular post. Describe your suitability for the post with particular reference to the criteria in the person specification. Include all relevant skills, knowledge and experience.**

2 RESETTLEMENT DEVELOPMENT WORKER (charity helping offenders)

Job Purpose

Encourage and assist women prisoners to meet their own resettlement needs by:—

    i   Providing a range of comprehensive information and materials for women and prison staff.

    ii   Helping prisons to meet the needs of prisoners by systems linked into the sentence planning process.

    iii   Encouraging and assisting prison staff to support self help and contact with families.

    iv   Helping community agencies and volunteers to deliver services to women in prison.

Person Specification

    i   Detailed knowledge of the prison system and internal structures, and understanding of resettlement needs.

    ii   Experience of working with women, including black women and women from varied ethnic backgrounds, and understanding of the principle of empowerment.

    iii   Experience of advice work and knowledge of housing and welfare rights legislation as well as the ability to train prison officers.

    iv   Ability to manage and facilitate use of computerised information systems.

    v   Ability to motivate prisoners, prison staff and volunteers.

    vi   Understanding of and commitment to equal opportunities.

    vii   Excellent communication and presentation skills.

    viii   Ability to work under pressure, on own initiative and as part of a team.

ix   Experience of setting up and evaluating new systems of work.
x   Ability to collect, organise and disseminate information.

Salary £14,837 pa.

Application Form

Personal Details, Current or Most Recent Job, Personal Career (CV- jobs, courses, qualifications)

Suitability for the Job

Tell us what makes you suitable for this particular post. Address each point of the Person Specification, giving details of what skills, experience and knowledge you have in these areas. Always be specific, make positive statements and do not use general phrases. The shortlisting panel needs to know how and why you think you can do the job.

Case Study of a Newcomer:– Tasneem (late forties).

The Job

Relationships counsellor and psychosexual counsellor; 45 hours one to one counselling and three to four case supervision groups per month; £8.50 ph for counselling.

Selection Process

1 Interview with a counsellor and a manager.
2 Sponsorship morning; personal interview and meeting other counsellors and possible candidates to talk and discuss subjects brought up by the counsellors.
3 One full day at headquarters; group discussions and 2 personal interviews.

Education and Qualifications

Certificate in Couple Counselling; 2½ years of theory (340 hours), skills, including groups and personal supervision (278-320 hours), and counselling practice (400 hours). Total Cost £3,000. Diploma in Sex Therapy; 200 hours client contact, 6 cases, and 3,000 word project. Total cost £2,500.

Household Context

Husband (high salary) and grown up children.

Satisfactions

The variety and challenge of working with different people. Helping and working with people as couples to look at possible ways of moving forward by understanding where they are coming from, why they feel and behave in certain ways with their partners, and to look at ways of changing should they wish to do so. Helping couples to express feelings and emotions when helpful and they had not thought possible.
In sex therapy working in a behavioural way with couples with sexual problems and dysfunctions that have impinged on their relationship. Helping them to work through these difficulties to result in a successful outcome.

Disappointments

Would like to have more supervision as part of the work conditions.

Surprises

Moving from counselling into sex therapy, which at the beginning of my counselling career I had not even looked at. It seemed a natural progression. Understanding of self which seems part of the counselling process.

Lucky Breaks
Ability to get into a new and stimulating career in my mid forties!
The Future
No further plans at present. To continue working as a relationship counsellor and sex therapist. To continue to play a part in the running of the counselling centre.
Advice
Bear in mind that the process of learning and being a counsellor opens up the self which previously had not been thought about. It can at times be painful but is also a wonderful learning process.
Comment
Tasneem is a good example of how to start a new career in mid life starting as a counselling volunteer, and also how to develop it in a new direction that she had not considered in the first instance.

Case Study of and Established Counsellor/Tutor:– Penny
The Job
1 Senior Health Education Officer/Counsellor (local authority), 31 hours per week, £21,000 pro rata. Training courses include bereavement and loss, counselling skills, women and sexuality, women and mental health, assertiveness, and equal opportunities.
2 Community and voluntary groups in mental health and women's health. With three others set up women's counselling service which now has 15 therapists/counsellors.
Selection Process
Interview with 2 members of staff.
Counselling and Related Training
1995-	Couple Counselling
1993-	Personal Psychotherapy
1991-93	Certificate in Counselling (university)
1989	Assertiveness Training
1989	Certificate in Adult Teaching
1987	Basic Counselling Skills and Groupwork Skills. Total Cost £7,500

Household Context
Self Employed Partner
Satisfactions
Autonomy (but it feels threatened); Working with client groups I like (the most disadvantaged); doing both multi agency training and 'in house' training; counselling in a free/low cost agency that I helped to set up.
Disappointments
The changing face of the NHS: their use of 'medical' and 'scientific' models for proof that counselling works; still lack of commitment from statutory agencies to provide this sort of support both to its own workforce and its clients.
Surprises
Self discovery on my own journey through therapy and supervision.

Lucky Breaks
Being in the right place: some students I was teaching told me about a part time job at the health promotion centre.

The Future
Plan to train as a psychotherapist; continue less than full time mix of training, unpaid work and possibly some private practice.

Advice
It helps to be in a caring profession. Get involved in a voluntary capacity which offers advice, helpline work or basic listening skills so that you can see if you are drawn to counselling.

Comment
Penny feels that her position is odd because it is not just counselling. However, there is no such thing as an 'ordinary' counsellor and training is a strongly related and compatible expertise. Given the cost of her own psychotherapy it is perhaps not surprising that she is keen to train is this area.

Case Study of a High Flyer - Craig (late 40s)
Work Experience
1991-	Independent Counselling Service – Coordinator.
	General Practice- Practice counsellor.
	Private Practice – Psychotherapist.
	Psychiatric Hospital – Honorary Psychotherapist/Staff Supervisor).
1986-91	Psychiatric Hospital – Head Social Worker.
	Psychotherapy Dept. – Introductory Course Leader.
	University – Student Counsellor.
1984-86	Hospital – Team Leader, Mental Health and Elderly.
1981-84	Clinic – Counsellor.
	General Practice – Counsellor.
	Social Work Student Unit – Supervisor.
	(All the above jobs are part time).
1981-83	Education Department – Counselling Course Co-Leader.
1977-81	Psychiatric Hospital – Social Worker.
1974-77	City – Social Worker.
1970-72	Charity Worker.
1967-70	Museum – Welfare Worker.

Education and Qualifications
1974	Social Work (CQSW).
1990	Analytical Psychotherapy.

The Job
Counselling Centre (south east England) – Coordinator, Approx. 10 hours per week. £800 per month.

Selection Procedure
Interview by Management Committee.

Counselling Training
Psychoanalytic Psychotherapy (£2,800).
Personal therapy over 5 years (£15,000)
Household Context
Married, part time salaried partner, 2 dependent children.
Satisfactions
Developing and improving a service: encouraging and helping volunteer counsellors to fulfill themselves: building upon existing training courses.
Disappointments
Working with the complex dynamics of volunteer counsellors without the necessary structure: this dissipates the energy of individuals and the organisation as a whole.
The Future
To develop the training programme so that it is comparable to the best in the region, and in parallel to improve the standard of counselling in the service.
Advice (for budding counselling centre coordinators)
Get trained and experienced: do get psychiatric experience if possible. Learn your own limits, be aware of them and work to reduce them.
Comment
Here is another counsellor with a 'portfolio' existence: Craig works currently in four different settings. His range of experience is helpful to his training role which fits comfortably alongside his counselling practice. This counselling centre is very small and unable to sustain any full time salaried staff but is still able to make a valuable service to the local community.

Conclusions

One striking feature of counselling the community is the importance attached in many jobs to equal opportunities and this can be interpreted in two ways. Applicants will be required firstly to demonstrate their awareness of cultural and other differences in the client population, and secondly their willingness to treat all clients with equal unconditional positive regard. Some counselling jobs are permitted (i.e. within equal opportunities law) to be restricted to particular candidates, notably women and/or ethnic minorities. Whilst the reasons for this are very understandable it could be argued that the underlying principle, that clients are ideally counselled by similar people, will disadvantage ethnic minority candidates who wish to work in a mainstream counselling job, i.e. where the majority of clients are white.

Such is the richness and diversity of counselling in the community that there are opportunities for just about everyone, paid or unpaid, full time or part time, to make a contribution. Your local County Social Services Department will have information about the opportunities for volunteers and related paid work. Some of these opportunities involve short term projects which reflects the uncertainty and change factors in employment discussed in chapter 1. In the event of a project being demonstrably successful then additional funding might be obtained to continue the good work which may become established in the longer term. Effective volunteers are often offered paid work.

CHAPTER 8:
CAREERS COUNSELLING

Introduction

According to Tony Watts (1994) careers guidance is currently higher on the public policy agenda than ever before. This is linked to profound changes which are taking place, both in education and in employment, in the relationship between the individual and the organisation. In particular the traditional concept of career and job for life is dying. Watts identifies changes in education in response to changes in the world of work including flexible learning, accreditation of prior experiential learning, modular courses, and replacement of grants with loans. More and more individuals are now operating a 'portfolio existence' in which they are engaged simultaneously on several different 'jobs' and this may prove especially to be the case with counselling. They think more carefully about education as a personal investment and their individual career decisions will also be shaped by household context: ie dependents, dual incomes etc.

Until recently careers work in higher education has been characterised by amateurism. I recall a seminar I ran at a conference in the mid 1980s at which many careers advisers cheerfully admitted they had little or no idea of theories of career choice and development. Imagine consulting a lawyer or doctor who had had no formal training in contrast to the many hours of counselling theory and skills required for BAC accreditation! I am pleased to report that there is now a Diploma in Careers Guidance in Higher Education at the University of Reading. In a variety of ways, especially training, education institutions are becoming more professional in their approach.

Definitions

Careers work is most often described in terms of 'advice' or 'guidance' and the relationship to counselling needs to be explained:–

1 **Careers 'Advice'**. This is the preferred term in most universities. Some careers advisers are keen to distance themselves from 'counselling' or 'welfare' which suggests that careers work is primarily about fitting up graduates with decent jobs in industry and the professions.

2 **Careers 'Guidance'**. Guidance is an umbrella term which encompasses counselling as well as activities such as informing, coaching, teaching and advocacy.

3 **Careers 'Counselling'**. This title is preferred by a small minority of British Universities. Interestingly at Harvard University in the USA the term 'career adviser' is reserved for Harvard Alumni who have agreed to act as helpful contacts for current students. The implication is that careers 'advice' is best given by practitioners of that career. Careers staff at Harvard are 'careers counsellors' and 'information managers'.

Many have trained in counselling but choose to work in a careers context. Others will have first level counselling skills, having trained in their Diploma in Careers Guidance courses to appreciate and implement Egan's famous model outlined in

'The Skilled Helper'. When I started work in Student Services, Oxford Polytechnic in 1981 the counselling service was fully integrated and therefore, having trained in person centred counselling, I was under-prepared for the fact that roughly half of my workload was 'careers'. I soon discovered that there was little fundamental difference between the two types of work. 90% of my 'personal' counselling clients saw me for four sessions or less and it was not unusual to see 'careers' clients for two or more sessions, especially the more anxious ones. A counselling approach to careers work is in my view both feasible and desirable.

A Client Centred Approach

Nathan and Hill (1994) identify four reasons why careers counsellors should not accept their clients' demands and expectations for advice on the best career:-

1 A rational decision will also need to address emotional issues such as relationships.

2 Lifelong decision-making skills are needed because there is no longer a 'job for life'.

3 Employers increasingly require employees to be be adaptable to change.

4 The client, not the counsellor, is responsible for making decisions because they are the experts.

They emphasise the *process* of careers counselling which enables people to recognise and utilize their resources to make career-related decisions and manage career-related

". . . change in the workplace"

problems. Help for young people had been well-established in the statutory careers services normally set in the education departments of local authorities, but help for adults was much more patchy and in some places non-existent. In the 1990s the government opened up careers to competitive tender and this led to more varied services with a major role being played by Training and Enterprise Councils (TECs). Some adult services were privatised and are now run on commercial lines with targets for different guidance services. In some counties the new agencies are doing a lot of adult work and even contract work with companies by offering fee paying career management services to employees. The distinction between public and private sectors in careers has become blurred to the point of being meaningless, and your effectiveness as a professional will be measured by sophisticated performance indicators whether you are accountable to local councillors, shareholders, private owners or civil servants. The various other professionals involved in helping others include careers teachers, human resource managers, outplacement consultants and occupational psychologists.

The Dept. for Education and Employment offer such schemes as the Enterprise Allowance, Job Clubs and Restart (primarily for unemployed people) but these are in a constant state of flux as central government responds to problems such as unemployment and skill shortages. The merging of these two departments means that job and training opportunities become more inextricably linked and the significance for counselling is that people will increasingly need lifelong guidance with all aspects of both work and education.

In addition to the armed services, many large organisations have career counselling programmes for some if not all of their staff. I was once involved in a day of counselling individual army officers as part of a six week course concerned with return to civilian life. I was struck by the enormous differences between officers of similar age and rank in terms of their self esteem, confidence, clarity of ideas, and skills of career choice. One officer had already turned down excellent jobs but another of similar rank was listless, lacking in direction, and perhaps needed counselling about his marriage.

Theories and Decision Aids

Nelson-Jones (1991) identifies four main theories of career choice and development:

1 **Developmental**. Super (1980) defines career broadly, including the main roles in life such as parent, homemaker, citizen and leisurite, played out in the main theatres of home and community as well as workplace. Careers therefore concern a lifetime of choice and decisions about work, love,and play.

2 **Behavioural**. Your chances in life are primarily determined by a combination of nature (genetic inheritance) and nurture (environment). Careers behaviour is largely conditioned by culture and circumstance.

3 **Differentialist**. This is the popular 'matching' theory of careers, based upon six personality types (e.g. practical, conventional) ideally searching for careers in one of six potentially matching types of environment.

4 **Structural**. This theory is based on the notion that your life chances are largely determined by your situation such as your family, your locality and your schooling.

Your own approach to career counselling will reflect your own attitude to these theories in much the same way as you contemplate the respective models of counselling. For example, a background in person centred counselling may suit a holistic and hence developmental approach, whereas devotees of cognitive behavioural models of counselling will tend to concentrate on behaviour change to achieve short term career goals. If you are working predominantly with people of few of no qualifications then matching theories will cut little ice. The dangers of stereotyping are legion and yet I am regularly reminded of the potential significance of a public school background, for example the confidence with which many such students approach careers in the City, and who is to say that confidence is misplaced?

The similarity with person-centred counselling is very noticeable in the following quote:–

"We believe that clients are very much the experts as far as handling their own problems are concerned. It can be easy for clients to give up their power to the careers counsellor, and adopt a passive approach to the 'expert advice giver' . . . The responsibility for decision making is therefore with the client, whilst the counsellor is responsible for facilitating the process . . . We see the entire career counselling process as facilitating the clients' resources to manage their careers more effectively." (Nathan and Hill: 9)

This view is strongly echoed in Watts (1995) who envisages a lifelong system that gives free access to information and limited guidance support, plus a range of costed services charged to those who can afford them. In the private sector careers consultants offer combinations of counselling and/or psychometric tests (abilities, personality). Clients tend to be impressed with batteries of tests, the results of which are then included in a report which concludes with the most promising courses of action and the most likely careers. Companies may employ outplacement consultants, as part of Employee Assistance Programmes (EAPs), which provide redundancy counselling and, more often, coaching and support in job-hunting.

Some careers counsellors make use of computerised occupational information and other careers guidance tools such as GRADSCOPE, a 39 item questionnaire and PROSPECT (HE), a more sophisticated software programme which allows the user to generate career ideas and compare them to their own 'profiles' of skills, values and interests. Educational and careers guidance units outside universities have a similar range of decision aids. The limitations of all these tools are fairly obvious and are certainly not a substitute for client decision-making. It is the client's values that drive the process and their skills and interests that dominate the matching with careers.

A Careers Encounter

Shireen is graduating in English Literature at a leading university and four days after her finals she is panicking. Her choice of A-level and degree subjects was straightforward, being based simply on interest and examination performance. What follows, rather than a verbatim account of their discussion, are my choices (as an observer) of Shireen's most significant statements and my careers counselling interpretation. The careers counsellor is Pam:

1. "I wouldn't have thought of coming to this university until a teacher said I could if I wanted to." A recurring theme is Shireen's dependence on significant others (teachers, parents and close friends) in making decisions.

2. "I haven't really got a clue." In reality we all pick up 'clues'. The issue is our awareness of them and how to interpret them.

3. "I've used PROSPECT but it wasn't much help." Shireen realizes that she doesn't have a distinctive profile of values etc. but this is not unusual.

4. "I want to do something that excites me." Her own work experience, like most students, is mundane and badly-paid and she is inclined to make inaccurate generalisations from this experience such as 'all office jobs are boring'. A theorist would diagnose inadequate 'opportunity awareness'.

5. " I have thought about journalism, advertising and public relations but entry to these careers is unstructured." The vast majority of english literature graduates want media-related careers and an old-fashioned careers adviser might be tempted at this point to dismiss these ideas, being tired of meeting starry-eyed students who want to present 'Blue Peter' or free-lance on the Sunday Times.

6. "I've never had a year out. I thought I might work (any old job) and save up to do a 4 week training course to teach english as a foreign language. Then I would travel and apply for the JET programme (teaching english in Japan)." There is a distinctive pattern here which is easily recognised by careers counsellors, TEFL being a popular choice for graduates who want the excitement of going abroad. For most it is not a long-term career choice.

7. "I realise that I am not so much choosing a life-long career as finding something to start from".

Shireen is starting to identify short and long-term career goals and her first job on graduation is highly unlikely to be her last. I would draw a number of conclusions from this encounter. With little prompting Shireen has identified no fewer than five possible careers which close examination will reveal display a disparate range of values, skills and interests. The optimum match with her personality and skills is by no means clear at this point. The transition from university to employment is much more complex, challenging and anxiety-provoking than that from school to university. Shireen is so far finding it hard to focus her well-developed intellect on the awesome task of deciding what of do with the rest of her life. Her current understanding of these five possible careers is woefully inadequate. She is also unaware of some important careers guidance facilities such as an alumni network which especially good at her university.

Careers counsellors like Pam, who has trained in psychodynamic counselling, rarely give advice to clients like Shireen: they do, however, give information which can be mistaken for advice. Shireen will make her own decisions on what to do next, such as arranging to meet an alumnus working in the diplomatic service, and she can make an appointment to see Pam again if she wishes. She now has a better understanding of the process of career choice and the realisation is dawning that this is a fascinating life-long process. It might surprise you to know that this brief encounter lasted all of 20 minutes!

Life Stage and Decision Making Problems

Nathan and Hill (1994) identify six life stages and their associated careers counselling issues:-

1 **School Leavers**. They want knowledge and guidance from the relatively unknown world of work.

2 **The Twenties**. People are faced with the task of leaving home and establishing their identity. Ideally they can try out different jobs.

3 **Age 30 Transition**. A time for re-assessment of careers and relationships.

4 **The Thirties**. The expectation is that people are settled in career, relationships and lifestyle.

5 **Midlife Transition**. There may be an acute recognition of the gap between aspirations and achievements (midlife crisis?). Women may be returning to a career after raising children.

6 **Forty-five Plus**. There may be a possibility of redundancy and the prospect of retirement begins to emerge. Calculated early retirement may enable a brand new career such as counselling to appear.

I have little experience of counselling the casualties of redundancy or 'downsizing' but one particular encounter springs to mind; I was asked to help a senior manager in his early forties caught in a management reorganisation. He had applied unsuccessfully for a job in the new scheme, they continued to pay his salary and gave him some work to do but of a mundane nature. I vividly recall him saying how he "had no idea how important power and influence were to him until they took them away". Victims of redundancy not uncommonly experience classical symptoms of loss and bereavement. Organisational change is but one of six types of change which can create problems according to Nathan and Hill (1995). The others are technological change, change in the nature of a job, change of boss, change in organisational values, and the liquidation of a small business. Sadly very many businesses fail, including some in counselling private practice. Other situations which might lead to referral for counselling or specialist legal help are unresolved personal issues in work-life balance, a pattern of chronic indecisiveness, and consideration of legal redress after discrimination.

Other decision-making problems which may be uncovered include pressure from third parties such as parents, inner conflict, possibly from values introjected from parents, fear of taking risks, preference for others to make decisions (so that they can be blamed when things go wrong), conflict between career and personal needs (e.g. job vs family), and fear of success simultaneously with fear of failure leading to paralysis. I have explored with groups of students the most likely reasons for *not* choosing a career and by far the most common was the desire to 'keep their options open' (therefore anything is possible). Others of significance included unreadiness to settle down, desire to 'take a year off', and the fear of making a mistake, all convenient forms of procrastination.

Training and Planning

Relevant qualifications and courses include:–

1   Postgraduate Diploma in Careers (or Vocational) Guidance. A degree or equivalent is normally required.

2   Membership of the Institute of Personnel and Development.

3   Reading University. Postgraduate Diploma in Careers Guidance in Higher Education.

4   Independent Counselling and Advisory Services. Counselling and Career Counselling Courses.

5   British Postgraduate Medical Federation. Career Counselling for Clinical Tutors.

6   Edgehill College of FE. Postgraduate Diploma in Counselling and Careers Work.

Other forms of training and experience which would be helpful include recruitment, training, personal and professional development, and, of course, mainstream counselling. Teachers can get involved in careers work at their schools. A colleague of mine trained in student counselling partly because she forecast, accurately as it turned out, that the popularity of her vocational subject would go into sharp decline. Another colleague considered doing a psychotherapy course in the 1980s in order to enhance his chances of moving later into private practice. I myself went out of my way to edit two counselling and careers newsletters respectively and published many articles, partly to improve my chances of being paid to write or edit. Invitations to counsel or write do not come out of thin air.

A Day in the Life of Gerard (51, a careers advisor in a large northern university)

9 am. Monday in November. Our weekly departmental business meeting is uneventful, and I lose interest in the protracted annual discussion about the venue for the office Christmas party. Much as admire my colleagues they do like to chat! I am more interested in the student feedback report on the annual careers convention.

10–12.30. It's my turn as duty careers advisor, a task I enjoy because of the sheer variety of encounters. I see no fewer than 20 students and recent graduates in the open plan office. Of course this is hopeless for confidentiality but this does not seem to trouble the students who raise all kinds of issues. The more trivial queries include the location of information ("the file 6 inches above your head"), "what is all this about a milk-round?" and where to sign on for psychometric testing sessions. More challenging include "I haven't got a clue where to start" (a common presenting concern), "what are suitable careers for someone like me?" (a complex matching process) and "I've heard that a degree in my subject (anthropology) is useless" (nothing could be further from the truth). I steer them into sections of the library, workshops, or individual appointments as appropriate.

Over a sandwich lunch which I take in my office I read the leader pages from our office 'Guardian' and then glance at the registration forms for this afternoon's clients. I often find it helpful to have advance warning of questions they want to raise.

1.30. Jennifer is fairly typical of a final year student of english literature, with her ambitions to work in either journalism or publishing. Not unusually she has does virtually nothing to demonstrate a *serious* interest in journalism and seems to be largely unaware that in publishing editors need business acumen. I renew my determination to conduct a small research project into arts students and fantasy careers (according to developmental theorists we abandon these at around the age of 10). I encourage her to take action, including attendance at our forthcoming insight into media training course.

2.00. Derek enters looking dishevelled and uptight. He has been unemployed for over a year after completing a masters course in environmental management. After a relatively successful but previously unfulfilling career as a computer programmer he has made 119 unsuccessful applications for jobs and wonders if his age (late thirties) is counting against him. I note that at least they did result in 19 interviews but he announces aggressively that they weren't suitable jobs anyway, usually because they involved too much use of computers. Derek has serious problems with his strategy and it is difficult to find a diplomatic way of pointing this out. I suggest that next week he brings in his CV and information on vacancies so that we can look at them together, and also invite him to identify potential employers with a view to a networking approach. Just as he leaves he blurts out that a friend claims that people with beards (Derek has a huge one) are discriminated against: what do I think? I fondle my own trim beard and reply that there is some truth in this, but not in the case of of the environmental agencies Derek would like to work for.

2.30. Cathy, a final year student of music and sociology, wants me to have a look at her CV and, as usual, I ask her what sort of people might be reading it. She doesn't know. It transpires that the CV is in relation to jobs of a temporary nature that she might get on graduation. She is evasive about long term aspirations and I proceed with a routine attempt to liven up her CV (the average student first draft CV is typically dull and seriously understating achievements). It is very important to her to work in selected locations in London and suddenly she announces that whatever job she gets must be secondary to her need to practice her singing for four hours a day! At last her true ambitions are revealed and I can do my best to help and encourage.

3.00. Ravi has recently completed an MSc in Electronics and Computing and immediately admits to lacking in confidence. It soon transpires that this is largely based upon a misconception that employers attach enormous significance to how much you know. Most do not but are concerned about the ability to learn and adapt, change being the only thing they confidently predict. In a matter of minutes Ravi's CV is transformed from a low key, apologetic document to one that is positive and yet equally truthful. This encounter is a classic example of morale-boosting.

3.30. I have some minutes to spare so I make a couple of calls to academics about forthcoming joint presentations to groups of postgraduate students. I am aware of my ambivalence about working in partnership with them: I feel quite strongly that we should but they can be so awkward. I have blocked out the next 90 minutes in order to clear my in tray and do some urgently needed updating of some occupational folders. Information is my weak spot and I have to make a conscious effort to compensate for it. I am horrified to come across materials that are hopelessly out of date.

5.00. Jean is a mature student (30) of psychology and sociology with an impressive track record including high grades, experience as school governor and local councillor (lib-dem). She has already attended our Myers-Briggs (psychometric) workshop and has focused her considerable intellectual powers on interpretation of the resulting career suggestions. As usual some of them can be simply dismissed, for example hospital management because of her intense dislike of the NHS internal market and we focus on her main ideas. They include personnel management (my own previous career) and counselling so she in much encouraged to hear about EAPs and other ways in which these occupations might be combined. At the very end of our lively conversation she casually announces that she is restricted in working locally and part-time because of her family commitments. Her husband is a scientist and there is apparently no question of him compromising *his* career. Can she 'have it all'? We arrange to meet again.

I reflect once again how much more I enjoy this work compared to the cut and thrust of management in manufacturing industry. It was through recruiting graduates for my own company that I came across university careers work and I have found the counselling certificate course that I completed many years ago enormously helpful in both individual and group work. I don't feel too old for further training, perhaps the Diploma in Careers Guidance in Higher Education, by distance learning.

Typical Jobs
1 Careers Guidance Officer (Private Consultancy)
Person Specification
Essential:– Diploma in Careers Guidance (or Vocational Guidance)
Knowledge of Information Systems
Counselling Skills
Ability to work in a team
Desirable:– Experience of Recruitment
5 Years of Varied Work Experience
Degree or Professional Qualification
Teaching Experience
Application Form
Personal Details; Education and Training; Work Experience; References. **Describe your skills and experience and explain how they relate to this post.**

2 Adult Education Advisor (Training and Enterprise Council)
Purpose of Job To advise adults on the full range of educational and career opportunities in the South West Region.
Person Specification
Essential:– Education to degree standard or equivalent.
Experience of recruitment or careers guidance.
Ability to establish rapport with a wide variety of clients.
Knowledge of relevant legislation including equal opportunities.
Desirable:– Training in counselling.
Experience of working with unemployed people.
Knowledge of psychometric tests.
Teaching experience.
Application Form
Personal Details: Education and Qualifications; Present and Previous Employment;

Activities and Interests; Other Relevant Information; Referees.
Explain how your skills and experience relate to this position. Please address your answer to each part of the job specification.

3 Director of University Careers Service (salary £30-35,000 pa)

The university, following a major reorganisation, is starting a phase of its development in which the careers service will have an enhanced role.

Person Specification

Essential:– Minimum of 10 years experience of careers work in further or higher education or graduate recruitment.

Professional qualification in careers, counselling, or human resource management.

Proven management ability.

Self starter.

Desirable:– Teaching experience.

Qualifications and experience of psychometric testing.

Experience of managing budgets.

Send full CV to The Chairman of the Appointments Committee.

1 Case Study of a Comparative Newcomer – Deepak (late 20s)

Work Experience

1994-   County Council – Careers Guidance Officer

1990-93 Manufacturer – Trainee Personnel Officer (recruitment)

1988-90   Health Authority – Medical laboratory science officer.

Education and Qualifications

1995-   University – Studying part time for certificate in counselling. Diploma in Careers Guidance

1988   Polytechnic BSc (hons.) in Biological Science.

1986   Polytechnic HND in Applied Biology

The Job

Generic careers guidance officer: salary £12,100 pa.

Selection Procedure

Panel Interview: group task (6 candidates have to decide on a course of action for a given scenario)

Household Context

Married, no children.

Lucky Breaks

Chance opportunity to be involved in recruitment (cover for maternity leave). This in turn helped me to get the careers job.

Surprises

The poor quality of written applications for jobs: discovering that the careers service would be taken over by the local TEC.

Satisfactions

Being thanked by people who have found my guidance helpful: mastering nerves when giving presentations to large audiences.

Disappointments
Low salary: working with young people whose prospects are minimal and they know it: no financial support for the counselling course.

The Future
Aim for careers advisor post in a university : complete a diploma in counselling at work (part time).

Advice to Budding Careers Officers
Get industrial and commercial experience first: practice your career counselling skills on any young people you encounter.

Comment
Deepak is on his third career already but has no regrets about the moves he has made because he finds all his experience useful. He is aiming to be well qualified in careers, counselling and also educational guidance which are likely to be growth industries for the foreseeable future.

3 Case Study of a Freelance Careers Guidance and Personal Counsellor – Sioban

Education and Qualifications
    1988   British Psych. Society Chartered Occupational Psychologist
    1979   Polytechnic. Cert. in Counselling (cognitive/behavioural)
    1968   University MSc in Occupational psychology.
    1965   University BA (Hons.) Psychology

Work Experience
    1989-   Freelance work
    1975-89   University Careers Advisor
    1973-75   Industry – Graduate Recruitment Manager
    1958-73   Commerce Personnel Manager

The Job
Chartered Occupational Psychologist in Private Practice in the south east of England: salary average £27,000pa: careers guidance and personal counselling: clientele includes people who are:
    * Reviewing career options
    * Women returners
    * Facing redundancy
    * Wanting coaching in applications and interviews

Selection Procedure
None, but offer of early retirement gave me the incentive.

Household Context
Divorced and living alone: lump sum invested enabled me to take a chance on private practice.

Satisfactions
Independence: take home pay now much higher than when at university: variety of clients most of whom are very appreciative of the service.

Disappointments
No colleagues to interact with.

Surprises

Earning as much as at university: discovering entrepreneurial flair.

Lucky Breaks

Being offered early retirement (unfortunately terms less favourable than redundancy): being encouraged by trusted colleagues when wavering about decision.

The Future

Carry on as now: perhaps seek office in profession: maybe write a book.

Advice to Budding Freelancers

Networking in advance of going into private practice in order to line up likely sources of referral: networking afterwards: obtain the highest quality of training and obtain a recognised professional qualification. don't set your fees too low (I charge £33-£45 per session with higher fees for aptitude and personality test/feedback): when in doubt trust your gut reaction.

Comment

Sioban has the qualifications and experience to be able to offer an attractive blend of skills to clients who are mostly well off and able to pay high fees.

Conclusions

I have no doubt that careers and educational guidance are valid sectors of counselling work. Working albeit very briefly with clients about what they are going to do with the rest of their lives is a fascinating and rewarding job, although I acknowledge that the vast majority of clients are not seriously troubled and therefore would not be seeking the services of a mainstream counsellor or psychotherapist. In the largest careers departments there may be some scope for specialising in 'special needs' clients, and the work is becoming more and more bound up with educational guidance which will throw up a wide range of clients, some of whom will present a challenge even to a versatile counsellor. I found that personal counselling is potentially more rewarding than career counselling but it is also much more stressful, one of the main reasons why supervision is vital. Along with work and medical settings, careers counselling and educational guidance could well become an area of significant growth.

CHAPTER 9:
COUNSELLING IN PRIVATE PRACTICE

Introduction

As I explained in chapter 2, private practice is seen by many counselling students and some employees as a very attractive career option and this does not surprise me in the least. The notions of being in full control of your destiny, perhaps working from home, eventually picking and choosing your clients and charging them substantial fees sound attractive. The most successful free-lancers can reasonably expect to become involved in training and, eventually, supervision. On the other hand it can be a lonely and risky business and it is significant that the majority of private practice counsellors have other related jobs and/or sources of income. Feltham writes convincingly (in Dryden 1995) on the stresses of private practice and is highly recommended reading before you even think of giving up the day job.

However, what is not in doubt is that since the 1970s there has been very rapid growth in public sector jobs such as in the NHS and further and higher education, and also in private practice. The reasons for this growth include the tendency for extended families to break down and also fewer people turning to the clergy and doctors. The latter professionals are now becoming increasingly counsellor friendly and are prepared to refer patients. Also the high quality of training available from organisations such as Relate and The Westminster Pastoral Foundation (WPF) will have tempted many to aspire to paid work.

Recently the BAC has set up a national register of counsellors (UKRC) which might lead eventually to Charter status, with four sections – humanistic/existential, psychodynamic/psychoanalytic, cognitive/behavioural, and eclectic. Syme (1995) eventually envisages a National Register of Counsellors, having two tiers of membership, for independent practitioners and employed counsellors respectively. The UKCP have similarly decided to form a Register of Psychotherapists which now checks that training is being properly validated and, given the legendary boundary disputes between different schools, is split into eight sections. 'Divide but rule' you might say.

Supply and Demand

Syme (1995) identifies four factors which account for the increase in demand for counselling:–

i   Rapid changes in the workplace resulting in less security and more stress.
ii   Preference for counsellors who are outside the client's workplace or social life.
iii Increased interest in alternative and holistic medicine.
iv   Disillusionment with drug treatment for depression and anxiety.

The number of BAC accredited members, mostly people who work at least part-time in private practice, grew by around 23% from 1991-94, whereas the number of students on advanced counselling courses rose in the same period by 58%. Private practice is a very popular setting in which to work but it will be difficult for inexperienced counselling course graduates to quickly build up their clientele, especially as those best suited to counselling are not usually natural entrepreneurs. I agree with Feltham (1993) that if you are the family's main breadwinner then you are well advised not to attempt to make a living from counselling. Private practice is best suited to otherwise well-established counsellors. Whatever your plan of action I would recommend conducting market research. As McMahon and Powell (1993) remind us:–

"Remember, the only reason businesses fail is because they run out of cash . . . We cannot emphasise enough how important it is to do this sort of calculation before you throw up your job and set up on your own."

Syme (1995) points out the uneven distribution in the private sector, especially the south-eastern bias also noted by the BAC. She concludes that for many parts of the UK the demand exceeds supply, such as in Northern Ireland, Cornwall and Cumbria where only three or four counsellors respectively were registered in the 1994 BAC Directory. It could be that where there are relatively many counselling jobs there will be fewer private practitioners. Derbyshire, for example, had only 11 BAC listed counsellors in the 1994 Directory but is one of the leading counties in the provision of counselling within general practices. Syme concludes that current demand for private practice exceeds supply (except in London) but Feltham (1993) does not think there are not enough clients to go round, and this is broadly confirmed by my own sample survey of BAC members. Competition may not be direct but it is subtle and it is there. One way to gauge it is to ask a friend or acquaintance who might be interested in becoming a client to ring up those private practitioners who are offering a similar service to the one you have in mind. A willingness to reduce fees and the absence of waiting lists would be prime indicators of a crowded marketplace. Alternatively they might all be very busy . . .

The USA Experience

In the USA most analysts and therapists are medically qualified and professional counsellors are required to have a degree in psychology, whereas in the UK few counsellors are psychology graduates. I was interested in a chapter written by Guy in 1987 in which he writes about 'Future trends in the Practice of Psychotherapy'. It makes rather gloomy reading because he regarded the golden era of psychotherapy as over at that time. It was no longer fashionable and, with decreasing numbers of clients and an increasing number of trainees, the market had become saturated. There had also been an alarming rise in the number of malpractice lawsuits. According to Syme (1995) the evidence from surveys in Great Britain and the USA suggests that clients are more vulnerable to sexual abuse than any other professional misconduct.

"Probably about 10% of practicing counsellors sexually abuse their clients." (Syme 82)

I assume that they were using a very liberal interpretation of the term 'abuse', but it certainly adds weight to the argument for a recognised profession, with codes of conduct, disciplinary procedures etc.

"10% counsellors actually abuse their clients"

Of course there are some significant differences in the respective health care and insurance systems, but Guy's commentary does to some degree resonate with the situation in 1996 in the UK. He argues that you will need to be very resilient and flexible to be successful and this is likely to include having other jobs and/or working in a group practice. Guy claims that there is a gradual move towards eclecticism which suggests that a wider range of approaches and techniques will be advantageous. On a brighter note he suggests two areas of likely growth in the future, namely work-related counselling and counselling in medical settings. This forecast coincides with findings in my survey of counselling course leaders and, given the impossibility of NHS or employers meeting all the potential demand for counselling, much referral to private practice can be anticipated.

Where to Counsel and Get Referrals

The advantages of group practice with others include sharing the running costs of premises, security of others in the building, mutual support and the possibility of peer supervision and cover. The obvious advantage of working alone is autonomy but that must be weighed against isolation and the financial burden of setting up and running a business. Many will use a room in their own home but there are several potential difficulties such as maintaining anonymity and family distractions. Ideally the premises offer a separate entrance, a separate telephone, a waiting room and a lavatory.

My own sample survey showed that the BAC Directory and GPs were two of the three best sources of referrals the third being, if you are very good, current or former clients. I also strongly recommend networking with friends and other contacts. A realistic aim would be to have no more than 5 sessions per day and 20 sessions per week with regular clients, because the work can be stressful. Some time should be set aside for returning old clients, administration, training, supervision, emergencies and possibly your own therapy. Often clients will work full-time so 8.30am and 5.00pm slots will be much sought after and an established practice may have a waiting list. Reasons for not taking on clients include people who are highly disturbed or potentially violent, or have personality disorders.

Successful independent counsellors have the luxury of more choice in who they see, unlike in employment. Most psychotherapists, psychodynamic and person centred counsellors can bank on long term clients whereas those using brief methods have a higher turnover and less predictable income. Clients tend to be white and middle class, but an increasing number of Afro-caribbean and Asian counsellors are developing a style of counselling appropriate to their cultures. It is important to 'look after yourself' which means arranging your own supervision, support and training. Many counsellors including Bramley (1996) remind us of the importance of working in cooperation with anyone giving the client medical treatment and to make this clear to the client when confidentiality is discussed. It is not unusual for two professionals to find they are in conflict about the care of a client. This is often generated by the client and a psychodynamic interpretation might indicate a replica of parents who were unable to cooperate over child-care.

Fees and Safeguards

Except in the cases of health insurance schemes and where the employer is paying such as in an EAP, then clients will be paying their own fees. The fees charged by BAC members in the 1994 BAC Directory were:-

   i   London – Median £28 p.h. (usually also' negotiable'), with a full range from £15 to £80 or, a sliding scale Median £20 to £30 , with a full range from £10 to £80.

"professionals . . . in conflict about the care of a client"

    ii Outside London – Median £22 (usually' negotiable'), or, on a sliding scale
       Median £20- £25.

Most counsellors are attracted to the work for other than financial reasons and some feel strongly that clients in need should be accommodated even if they cannot pay the going rate. Sliding scales, fee bands, concessionary rates and free places are possibilities and in practice most fees are negotiable. Factors which you can bring into account include experience (e.g. trainees normally charge less) and political ideologies: some may charge no fee but request a donation to charity. Clients may well value themselves more when they give time *and money* to counselling. If you tend to feel guilty about charging you might find it helpful to remember that in the unhappy event of marital breakdown your solicitor with charge upwards of £70 per hour, and consultancy fees for a wide range of comparable expertise starts at £200 per day.

    The following factors will need to be taken into account when setting fees. Overheads will include:–

    i   Supervision, training, personal therapy, professional meetings and associated travelling.
    ii   Subscriptions to professional associations, books and journals etc.
    iii   Telephone, answerphone, postage,stationary, advertising and possibly secretarial help.
    iv   Insurance (professional indemnity policy, loss of earnings), pension scheme.
    v   Running costs of premises (heating, lighting, water, cleaning, repairs).
    vi   Possible rental or mortgage of premises and council tax.

When you see a list like the above it acts as a reminder of the many things we take for granted in orthodox employment. It is normal procedure when a private home is being used to calculate a percentage of the running costs of the whole house and this will enable you to reduce your income tax. Perhaps all this information helps to explain why, according to my sample surveys reported in chapter 1, BAC accredited members in 1995 were earning on average only £8,800 pa. from counselling. It comes as no surprise to learn that the majority of them are mature women with other part-time jobs and/or salaried partners.

    The working year may be as few as 40 weeks after allowing for holidays of counsellor and clients, cancelled sessions and minor indispositions. Counsellors vary in their policies towards charging for time spent on the telephone or reading letters. You might consult an accountant when first starting to be self-employed and also inform the Inland Revenue and DSS. It is essential to keep accurate and up to date records and have a separate bank account. The situation in much more complex for a formal partnership and legal advice is recommended.

A Day in the Life of Kate (48)

Kate is a well established counsellor in full-time private practice, working from home now that her children have left.

Patrick. This is my fifth session with Patrick (47), a university lecturer: a very likeable man, self referred and recently recovered from a serious bout of depression. During his slide into depression he steadfastly and apathetically refused any form of counselling but was now willing to consider what had caused it. Superficially our sessions have gone well with Patrick only too willing to talk about his troubles, especially the legacy of guilt from his failed marriage and the refusal of his three children to accept his new partner, but he is very prone to intellectualisation which I invariably find unhelpful. He has also read a couple of textbooks on counselling and depression and I get the feeling he is going to grade as well as review my therapeutic performance after the initial contract of 6 sessions. This may produce a kind of confrontation for which I suspect Patrick will go to great lengths to avoid.

Betty. This is my second session with Betty, a 78 year old widow whose anxious son is paying for her counselling. It is obvious that she is here primarily to please her son, something she has been doing for the last 54 years. She suffers from a lot of pain, following what sounds like a botched operation, and has become something of a hermit. A devout Presbyterian, she now very rarely goes to church or to her other favourite activities, claiming that it is uncomfortable to sit for as long as an hour and she does not want to draw attention to herself by either taking a cushion or walking out. She is already treating me like her only daughter, more concerned for my welfare than her own.

Jack. Jack (39) is a part-time trainee counsellor who is seeing me as part of his training. He is disillusioned with his social work career mainly because he feels that he is applying 'sticking plaster' to society's problems. Recurring themes in our sessions have been his rather obsessive concern with his health and his poor upbringing. Although his father died when Jack was 12 years old, he has virtually no memories of him as a well man. He was seriously ill from TB when Jack was only seven and then spent months in hospitals and sanatoria before spending his last two years at home as an invalid. His father was a pharmacist who, it transpired, had foolishly dosed himself with medication and refused to see a doctor until it was too late for successful treatment. My suggestion that Jack felt that his father had been responsible for his

"Some clients are hard to like", even for good listeners

own premature death produced floods of tears and the anger stored up for 25 years poured out. His mother had constantly referred to how similar Jack was to his father, of whom she always spoke in glowing terms. I wonder how much anger Jack's mother might have stored up.

Miriam. Miriam (47) has been seeing me for four months during which her attendance and punctuality have been erratic. She has been suffering on and off with depression for many years and has already exhausted the (time) limited counselling service of her GP. I seem to be her last resort. Her sister tragically died in a road accident six years ago and, although it was not Miriam's fault, because she was at the wheel at the time she tended to blame herself. This exasperates her husband and son who cope badly with her moods. She tearfully recalls a time when she had a dreadful row with her sister over a brief and reckless affair that Miriam had had with her brother in law. The incident was never mentioned again, and now she had lost for ever the opportunity to fully apologise: unfinished business.

Charles. Charles (27) who is very bright, charming, deeply cynical and yet amusing, is mysteriously unable to complete his Phd in biochemistry. I particularly enjoy my sessions with him because I allow myself to take risks, play hunches which often prove productive, and there is much laughter in spite of the seriousness of his situation. A glittering academic career is in jeopardy. I feel free to use my Gestalt training, which itself appeals to the theatrical side of my personality, and I tell him spontaneously about my fantasies (non-sexual!) about him. In just three sessions the advantages (or 'pay-off') of his procrastination are becoming apparent, such as his need to sustain secret ambitions to be a travel writer or a bass guitarist in a rock band. I end the session in fine mood and ride my bike to my supervision group.

Supervision. I enjoy supervision in spite of (because of?) the fact we are a very odd group. We tend to disagree a lot between ourselves not least because we have such different backgrounds and philosophies. My fondness for Gestalt irritates the cerebral Graham whose heavily into Jung, but not so Val who cheerfully admits to extreme eclecticism: she will call upon *any* theory or technique to make her clients better. Shona is psychodynamic, very sceptical of Val's methods, and I greatly admire her for her work which is mostly with patients newly diagnosed with degenerative and terminal illness. Our supervisor William, who says practically nothing, is a complete mystery to me, and a fly on the wall (even one with some counselling training) would wonder what he was doing there. He is an analyst (I try hard not to hold that against him!) and this week my report of progress with Miriam produces a faint smile. I don't know how he does it but our group works very well and we must be the only counselling supervision group to repair to the pub afterwards to argue about our various sporting interests. By the time I get home I have switched off from my clients, and the dog, as always is delighted to see me. If only all my clients could be like that . . .

Case Study of a Comparative Newcomer to Private Practice:– Megan (late forties)
Education
University:– BA (Hons) in History: Diploma in Education.
Counselling and Psychotherapy Training: Institute of Group Analysis: Relate

Certificate in Couple Counselling: Additional Training in Groupwork, PR.
Therapy:– Two 90 minutes sessions per week of group therapy over 4 years.
Later this year I hope to receive UKCP accreditation. I am considering applying for
BAC accreditation.

Work Experience

Teaching History
Teaching English as a Foreign Language (Germany – Married to Army Officer)
Counselling Some Service Personnel
Career Break (children)
Part-time Teaching and Adult Education
Part-time Teacher of R.E
Committee Member of Psychotherapy Society (unpaid)

The Job

From 1993 Private Practice, building up to 20 ongoing clients and 3 groups. Also a
few hours and/or sessions for:–

i   Counselling at an Independent School.
ii   Teaching Introductory Counselling Course.
iii Long-term Group (University).
iv   Teaching in Counselling and Issues of Faith.
v   Counselling in a General Practice.
vi   Facilitate Group of Trainees in Local Counselling Centre.
vii Group Work and PR Work for Relate.

Now at the point of being able to decline work.

Selection Procedure

My only selection procedures were for training.

Household Context

Single Parent with 2 grown up children.

Satisfactions

The intense nature of the work uses all of me.

Disappointments

Extra year of training in groupwork required.

Surprises

Being invited to teach counselling .

Lucky Breaks

Right place at right time (Relate needed part qualified counsellor). General practice
went fund-holding at the right time.

The Future

Further develop counselling and issues of faith. Educational role in group analysis
(including international dimension). Writing a counselling text book for introductory level
and as contributor to analytic theory as suggested by the experience of clinical work.

Advice to Budding Private Practitioners

If you are getting consistent and positive feedback about yourself as counsellor, then
persist, think laterally, slog along on the 'bottom deck'. Be open. Work on your own
'warts'. Have a second string to your bow.

Comment

Within the last 12 months Megan has earned money from no fewer than 8 sources, including work that covers 4 BAC Divisions. As is so often the case, when her own career was interrupted by her husband's posting overseas, she adapted to her situation and developed new skills and experiences. Having a 'second string to your bow' was something of an understatement. Training and counselling clearly fit comfortably together and writing would seem a logical development.

Case Study of an Established Counsellor:– Roberta (50s)

Work experience

1988   Full-time Self-employed in Private Practice.

1980-88 Part-time Self-employed Counsellor: Founder Member of Women's Centre: Some College Counselling.

1982-88 University – Part-time Assistant Student Counsellor.

1979-80 College of Higher Education – Student Counsellor (personal and vocational). Teaching and Tutoring Experience includes Counselling Skills (community education), Workshop Leader for Themes including Body Image, Stress, Bereavement and Relationships. Regular Lecturer on Introduction to Counselling Course: Ad-hoc Tutor for e.g. Women's Group (university) and Psychotherapy Course for Nurses.

Also 1960-1982 University – Field Interviewer, Care Officer, Research Assistant, Secretarial/PA and Editorial Work

Education and Qualifications

Several years of Personal Therapy which has Formed the Basis of Practice. Accredited to BAC for 5 years: Committee Member of Local BAC Branch. Several Training Courses attended in last 5 years.

1983-84 Institute of Group Analysis- Certificate in Group Work and Family Therapy (1 year part time)

1977-79 Assn. for Training in Counselling – 4 hours per week, 2 year Course.

1978-79 University Postgraduate Diploma in Counselling.

1972-75 University – MA in Psychology with Philosophy.

The Job

Self-employed, average 15 sessions per week working from home (long-term psychodynamic). Also short-term work with organisations for counselling in industry. Main sources of referral are BAC Register, GPs and industrial counselling agencies. I hold personal indemnity to the value of £500,000 (costs £40 pa): industrial agencies now recommend £1,000,000 insurance owing to 'abuse' problem.

Selection Process (for clients)

Exploratory first session to see if both want to continue: weed out those who don't want to work. Do not see people on drugs or those who could see a specialist e.g. anorexia.

Household Context

Single

Satisfactions

People get better! Using important parts of self: i.e. rational, emotional, intuitive. Self employment gives scope and freedom.

Disappointments

Some very difficult clients who turned out to be more disturbed than originally assessed: can be stressful: also threats of violence (only once) are a shock after some good work done. Severe disruption of practice when moved house although in same town: numbers dropped substantially and some clients quite disturbed. Too many counselling trainees in the locality are driving down fees.

Surprises

Learned and developed a lot. The value of personal counselling, experience and 'compatible' supervision (recent BAC guidelines stress importance).

Lucky Breaks

Research assistant job at hospital after degree in psychology. Job following training placement in same college (provided valuable reference). Then 'hanging about' for right job led to ideal experience as assistant counsellor at university.

The Future

Turning towards writing (creative mainly). Becoming more aware of the value of other theoretical positions.

Advice for Budding Private Practitioners

Check with BAC about accreditation requirements before you select training: number of study hours can be crucial. Get properly qualified for yourself: ie exactly what you want to do after a general accredited counselling course. Also get qualification recognizable by the general public. Stick to your guns about what you want to do which will result in self development. It is a good job and is valuable personally, but it is also demanding. It is not very lucrative and is a difficult area to be a high flyer.

Comment

Roberta belatedly seized the opportunity to graduate as a mature student and enjoyed an immediate break into the mental health field. This in due course enabled her to develop a professional career in counselling. As with many private practitioners she has a parallel role in teaching and tutoring which is important given the difficulties of earning a living from private practice alone.

Case Study of a Private Practitioner Turned Academic:– David

Work Experience

1995-	University Senior Lecturer in Counselling
1993-95	EAP Regional Manager (part-time)
1994-95	University Student Counsellor (part-time)
1991-94	NHS Trust Counselling Course Director (university accredited)
1991-93	Counselling Consultants – Consultant
1991	Alcohol Treatment Centre – Senior Counsellor (locum)
1986-93	Freelance Counsellor, Trainer and Supervisor
1987-90	Mental Health Charity – Senior Counsellor/Client Support Worker
1981-87	Probation Hostel- Senior Counsellor/Deputy Warden

Education and Qualifications

1987-92	BAC Accredited Counsellor
1988	Msc. in Psychological Groupwork (Polytechnic)

| 1981 | Postgraduate Diploma in Counselling in Educational Settings (University) |
| 1977 | M Theol. (hons) Divinity & Practical Theology (University) |

Teaching /Training Responsibilities

1995	College Tutor (part-time)
1995	College Workshop Presenter
1992-93	Counselling Centre – Counselling Tutor
1990-92	University – MSc Supervisor
1990-92	Training Programme Supervisor, Trainer
1990-92	Mental Health Organisation – Counsellor Supervisor
1985-92	Charity, Probation Service, Health – Freelance Trainer & Group Facilitator, Authority, D O Health, University etc.

Professional Activities

| 1987-95 | Include External Examiner (twice), Diploma Course Consultant, Dissertation Reader, Referee for Journal Articles, Publisher's Referee for Book Proposals, BAC Conference Workshop Organiser, Founder/ Coordinator of Counselling Centre. |

Research

| 1990-91 | University- Pilot Project – Clients' Experience of Counselling |

Publications

2 Books published by self, and 7 others as co-author.
1 Book in Press Edited by Self, and 5 in preparation (3 by self and 2 as editor).
2 Chapters Published and 2 in Preparation.
4 Times Series Editor (2 already commissioned and 2 in preparation).

The Job

University Lecturer in Counselling, Pay £26,223 pa.

Selection Procedure

Panel Interview

Household Context

Salaried Partner (full-time), 2 dependent children.

Satisfactions

Past – counselling practice, and autonomy of private practice.
Present: – Variety of challenges. Enjoy prospect of belonging to an organisation after the wilderness and insecurity of freelance work.

Disappointments

Past: – Conflicts with manager: pressure to manage and sell counselling and doing relatively little actual counselling.
Present: – Internal politics: Pressure to generate income: temporary contract.

Lucky Breaks

Getting into lucrative EAP work: getting consultancy contract partly through experience and knowing someone: knowing some leading figures in the counselling world. Current job: right place right time.

The Future

Establish myself academically: need more money: be involved in improving counselling and also putting counselling into context: decent standard of living more important than status.

Advice to Budding Private Practitioners/Academics

It may take a long time: get yourself well (plurally) qualified: take on various voluntary and paid kinds of work in counselling: get to know a lot of people by networking: teach, supervise and write: be visible: believe in yourself: be hungry for success: prepare to be criticised and envied: take risks.

Comment

Now is the time to reap the benefits of a lot of hard work and perhaps have more secure and predictable income. Unfortunately David is on a temporary contract but that is now the norm. I have often come across this bland assertion of' being in the right place at the right time' but he most certainly did not get the lecturing job by chance.

Conclusions

The optimism of counselling students about working in private practice is not reflected in the views of current private practitioners or by counselling course leaders, because it looks likely that graduate numbers will increase at a faster rate than those of available clients. Furthermore, I doubt the wisdom of relatively inexperienced counsellors working freelance. I would have thought that private practice was more appropriate when counsellors have established themselves in their communities and, through networking, have maximized the potential for referrals via GPs, employers, colleagues and others. Many counsellors are not natural entrepreneurs and this is reflected in the fact that most have other sources of income. The most successful private practitioners are likely to be involved in training and supervision which helps them to establish a strong local reputation. They have no need to advertise and may be in the comfortable position of referring clients to others including their own supervisees. Like other professional activities counselling in private practice is subject to the discipline of the marketplace.

However, if you like to take risks and are confident in your abilities private practice remains a very attractive option and you can always hedge your bets by initially combining it with more secure part-time employment. What could yet prove to be very significant is the fact that the two settings that are most likely to grow (medical and work) are themselves prime sources of private clients. Private practice is the acid test: if you are good you will survive, if you are very good then you will thrive. Are you ready to take that chance?

CHAPTER 10:
YOURS QUESTIONS ANSWERED

1 *I am qualified and I don't know whether to apply for accreditation or for a master's degree; which would better enhance my career?*
I would normally place accreditation well ahead but the exception might be in higher education. I suggest that you ask some chairpersons of selection committees for the types of job you have in mind.

2 *I don't know whether to do this three year part-time counselling training or a three to four year psychotherapy training. Which is more useful to my career?*
Psychotherapy is slightly more flexible and better for long term work, but often more expensive. In private practice there is the added advantage that your workload is more predictable and stable. Psychodynamic counselling, with thorough personal therapy would be a reasonable compromise.

3 *I want to go into private practice. What minimum training must I have?*
There are none as far as I know, but I would suggest a BAC accredited course (or equivalent) plus a minimum of five years full-time equivalent experience before you even consider it.

4 *The trainers tell me this course is nationally validated, but not by BAC; how valid is it?*
It could be the UKCP (the psychotherapy equivalent) or any of the many bodies listed in the BAC Training Directory. It simply means that you have completed the minimum requirements of training and therapy and experience as determined by that body, some of which are better known and established than others.

5 *As an experienced counsellor, should I take the risk of early retirement from my job and go into private practice, or would I be better off seeing out my time in the job?*
You cannot normally take early retirement until you are 50 except on health grounds. You might compromise by negotiating a part-time contract with your employer as private practice might take a while to build up. You would probably be better off seeing out your time but I notice that many of my case studies are successful risk-takers.

6 *I've heard that opportunities in counselling have bottomed out. How can I can I know if this is true?*
You could survey a sample of potential employers and private practitioners in your locality. Ask them whether or not they expect growth of counselling work in the next five years.

7 *I want to work in the AIDS/alcohol/primary care/university etc field. What is the best route for me (training etc); are there specialist courses?*
There are courses for most settings and for many issues but many of them are in

London. The supervised placement is an opportunity to get particular experience and voluntary work with built in training might be useful. Consult BAC's journal 'Counselling' and contact organisations in those fields you are interested in: ask their advice.

8 *I am doing a basic certificate in counselling; can I get CATS points from this towards qualifications in my nursing career?*
In principle yes. Your counselling course can be measured against this baseline for CATS points. Your nurse training adviser would have to consider the similarity of your course to counselling training for nurses such as:– Counselling in Caring Relationships for nurses, midwives etc, A06 98:– Principles of Psychosexual Counselling, N21:– Genetic Counselling in the Community. There are also courses with a significant counselling element such as Stress Management (N12), Problem Drinking (963), Substance Abuse (962), AIDS/HIV (44) and Care of the Dying and their Families (931). These courses range from 10 to 30 days.

9 *Would I be better off doing a psychology degree and aiming to become a clinical psychologist, rather than a counsellor?*
Clinical psychology, which takes six years of training, has two current advantages over equivalent counselling qualifications: firstly it is an established, recognised profession with jobs built into the NHS and private sector: secondly it equips you to work with a wider range of clients/patients including mental illness and severe disturbance. By comparison counselling courses are often a mix (sometimes an exotic mix!) of elements of psychology, sociology, theology and philosophy. Psychologists' reports may be recognised by the courts when counsellors' are not, and some private health companies will refer to psychologists but not to counsellors.

10 *How much does it really cost to train to become an accredited counsellor (including supervision, continuing professional education, accreditation application, memberships, professional insurance etc)?*
I estimate the initial cost of qualifying in the region of £5,000 and annual running costs around £1,500, without taking into account income tax relief or any lost earnings to attend training/supervision. I have included estimates for travel during the training period, maintaining a room at home (for private practice) and ongoing personal therapy. The total costs for analytic psychotherapy will probably be much higher.

11 *I have been a social worker for twenty years; surely I don't have to go and do another three years training to become a counsellor?*
I am afraid it may well take that long because most BAC accredited courses are two or three years (part-time). Legally there is nothing to prevent you from setting up in private practice with only minimal top-up counselling training, but it would be difficult to get employment as a counsellor.

12 *I qualified three years ago and I want to be a supervisor and trainer; what do I have to do?*

There are over a dozen training courses for budding supervisors listed in the BAC Training Directory. I would also suggest that you consult your own supervisor and/or mentor about making this move. Then you would need to attract your clientele by marketing and networking. Are you confident that three years post qualification experience is really enough?

13 *I've heard that there are scholarships for black people to train as counsellors (I'm black); is this true?*
I have not heard of this scheme but I know who would know: the chair of Race, the newest and smallest BAC Division. You can contact her via the BAC in Rugby.

14 *I've heard it said that if you have a chronic or recurring illness you can't be a counsellor because you've got to be consistently available for clients; is this true?*
No, it's not literally true but you have to be realistic about caseload. The BAC code of ethics states quite clearly that counsellors should not counsel when their functioning is impaired by circumstances including illness. Psychodynamic counsellors should not be frequently ill because this would harm their work and people with ME would tend to get exhausted. Employers in medical settings will very carefully check your state of health.

15 *I've been sending off job applications for the last four years and I rarely get shortlisted; am I doing something wrong? How can I find out?*
You are at least getting interviewed occasionally, bearing in mind that for an average counselling job only one in four get that far. I am quite certain that you can improve your application skills by seeking expert advice. You could start by asking for constructive feedback from your next unsuccessful application. You might even track down the successful candidate, identify the job they are about to vacate (and apply for it), and ask what is the secret of their success.

16 *I only have a few O-levels and I am not particularly academic but I am interested in counselling. Do I have a reasonable chance of qualifying and getting work?*
'A few O-levels' puts you in the top 25% of academic ability so you can start by not putting yourself down. You must develop a serious interest in counselling theory or you will never qualify, and you can put yourself to the test by reading McCleod (1993) or Feltham (1995), especially the more academic bits. If you are blessed with natural ability and enthusiasm then you will get work.

17 *I want to be a student counsellor but I have only worked in residential social work since my counselling training; how can I get into student counselling?*
You too can stop putting yourself down; after all you do have valuable relevant experience of working with young people. Read Bell (Open University Press, forthcoming) which is about counselling in further and higher education.

18 *I am an experienced counsellor but my career suffered because a client made a complaint against me; how can I explain this on my CV or when I get an interview?*

Every professional counsellor without exception has had dissatisfied clients although mercifully few lodge formal complaints. Decide how much, if any, of this complaint was justified and address the question of what you are doing about it. An obvious choice would be to take it to your supervisor or therapist. If you insist on including it in your CV then I suggest you place it near the end and write in an 'antidote': for example, "I have learned a great deal from this situation". I'm not convinced you have to disclose this negative and therefore unhelpful information at interview, but if you feel you must then take great care with your body language and what exactly you say. Preferably you sit up, look them in the eye and explain how you have benefitted from this painful experience.

19 *I've heard that the only way you can really get on in counselling is by knowing the right people; is this true?*
No it's not, because there are other ways. However, there is a large grain of truth in this if you interpret 'knowledge' in the context of networking. It's not so much 'who you know' as 'who knows you'.

20 *I'm confused about counselling training since most diplomas seem to specialise in one approach (e.g. psychodynamic, person centred etc); what is the best one to do?*
I suggest you trust your instinct in your choice of training and you might bear in mind that the most common approaches in Britain are psychodynamic and person centred. Fortunately the legendary antagonism between different schools has receded over the years and eclectic and integrated approaches are much more widely accepted these days. Also I have noticed that for many jobs there is a preference for candidates with knowledge of more than one approach. Perhaps avoid anything too novel, exotic or unproven.

21 *I want to emigrate and work in the United States; is it true you need a PhD to work as a counsellor or therapist?*
No it's not, although it is easier to circumvent their immigration rules if you are very highly qualified. You should bear in mind that American counsellors usually do have at least a Master's (although the standard may be closer to a British diploma). I have no doubt that psychology is the most useful first degree to take and chartered psychologist status should be very useful. I understand that requirements vary from state to state and from profession to profession. Check with the relevant professional bodies such as the American Counselling Association.

22 *I'm a recovering alcoholic and an alcoholism counsellor (NADAC); I want to start some general counselling. Do I have to do extra training and if so what?*
Your training with NADAC, however worthy, is insufficient if you want to work in the mainstream or in a different setting.

24 *I've retired, I'm 60 and want to be a counsellor, but I understand that some training institutes are against older students; is this true?*
I am delighted to report that my own sample survey found no evidence of ageism,

except at the lower end of the scale where the lower age limits of 25 or 30 are sometimes stipulated. Some psychotherapy training, because of its length and other requirements, may present difficulties.

25 *What is the advantage of doing a BAC accredited course?*
The short answer is the promise of quality. In many established professions only accredited courses survive, especially where they are delegated to universities. External examination and quinquennial review of courses in higher education are now standard practice in most universities or comparable institutions and quality control is here to stay. Under these circumstances is it surprising that many people will assume, perhaps unfairly, that accredited courses are better? In turn they are likely to attract the best tutors.

26 *I have got a psychology degree; would I be better off pursuing BAC accreditation or BPS counselling psychologist status?*
This is a tough one because the latter is so new that it is difficult to gauge progress. Some NHS clinics may be able to employ counselling psychologists but not counsellors because of their internal rules. I suggest you conduct your own survey of the most likely prospective employers. Firstly you have to identify the type of vacancy that would appeal to you and then mail them a simple and brief questionnaire. Use devices that make it very easy to respond like tick boxes, space to add comments, an SAE and you will get a decent response rate. When you get your result please send me a copy as I would be interested to know!

27 *I want to work in a meaningful one to one way with people and I think I am a good listener, but I don't believe in all this accreditation nonsense. Can I still be a counsellor?*
Yes of course you can and you will swell the ranks of people who are unhappy or unconvinced by the rigorous BAC accreditation process. However, there is more to being a competent counsellor than a few skills and lending a sympathetic ear.

28 *I have a criminal record; will this prevent me from becoming a counsellor?*
For most jobs 7 years is the period you must serve before your conviction is regarded as 'spent', but organisations that work with children such as the NSPCC are exempt from the Rehabilitation of Offenders Act 1974 and all subsequent amendments. If your conviction might impinge on counselling work (e.g. for sexual indecency) you should consider disclosing this if interviewed. This may affect BAC membership.

29 *I have a disability; where can I train as a counsellor?*
The Westminster Pastoral Foundation (London) run part-time courses in Counselling Skills and Attitudes for Deaf Trainees in (two years for certificate, three years for diploma). Manchester University run a two year part-time Certificate in Counselling Skills for Deaf People. Many of the institutions in the BAC Training Directory (BAC 1993) indicate whether or not there are facilities for people with disabilities, wheelchair access, and whether other special needs can be considered. A few openly welcome disabled students.

30 *I'm really serious about making it as a counsellor and I don't see why I shouldn't make good money at it; any ideas?*

In the employed sector there are some quite well paid senior positions such as head of student services at a prestigious university (around £40,000 pa). Networking with the counsellors who charge the highest fees (see the BAC Directory) would enable you to find out what is the secret of their success, assuming they are prepared to tell you. Engaging in pioneering research, preferably at a prestigious university, and subsequently writing books is bound to make your reputation and keep the royalties flowing. You would need to work long hours and/or charge high fees in private practice to earn a lot. Some practitioners who combine paid roles (e.g. lecturer) with private practice, running workshops and offering consultancy, earn very highly. Employee counselling can potentially pay very well as can training offered commercially. One commercial counselling organisation reputedly sold for approximately £4 million and there is anecdotal evidence of some single-minded practitioners earning over £60,000 pa. If you are entrepreneurial the sky is the limit.

CHAPTER 11:
CVS, APPLICATIONS AND INTERVIEWS

Introduction

First the bad news: the average number of applicants for counselling jobs is over 20 and rising. The good news is that up to one third of them fail to meet the minimum criteria and/or are so badly presented that they stand no chance. Around another one third have the relevant qualifications and experience but their approach is low key and/or stuck at the level of bland description. The readers of these CVs or application forms have no way of knowing anything about the *quality* of the applicant's experience or that there may have been some excellent outcomes if they are not told. The remaining one third or so will have a realistic chance because their approach is both positive and tailored to the particular job on offer, and the best three to six will be invited for interview. One or more of these may fail to maintain this high standard in person so, if you are keen and well prepared, then your chances are actually quite good.

For years I have mused over the reasons why so many well educated people such as graduates present themselves so poorly. I think part of the explanation is that academic courses train you to describe phenomena in a detached, objective way. Students are conditioned to write 2,000 word descriptive essays and reports which are very different to 250 word statements on why an employer should give you a job. I have even witnessed an academic describe self analysis, an essential element of career choice, as 'unhealthy navel gazing'. In some ways I admire classic British reserve and understatement but not when it comes to getting a job.

CV Design

Some people will advise you to leave out some parts of your CV or application form because they will appear either in your references or your own covering letter. In my view this could be a big mistake, firstly because your references may not even be requested until after shortlisting, and, secondly, the main assessment of your case will very likely be determined by the quality of the CV/application form. Of course, a well drafted covering letter can indeed enhance your case by complementing the main document but it is risky to 'relegate' some of your best material to what is a secondary document. The following sample CVs illustrate a range of approaches. As you read them ask yourself what impressions are you forming about the the applicant? I assert that the stages of CV and written application are indeed largely impressionistic and therefore your task is clear: you must create a good impression and initial impact is crucial. What are your impressions of the following three candidates?

CV – Jane Elizabeth Moran

Personal Details: Address
    Sex: Female
    DOB 1943   Marital Status: Single

Education:
    Secondary School: O-level: English (C), Maths (C), History (C)
    1954-61   English Lit. (C), Geography (D), CSE: Chemistry
                                 (2), French (3), A-Level: Geography (C), Economics
                                 (D), History (E)
    University: 1961-65   BSc. Sociology (2i). Dissertation: Single parenthood
                                 and job discrimination.
    College of F E: 1985-91   Introduction to Counselling. Certificate in
                                 Counselling.
    Polytechnic: 1980-83   Diploma in Management Studies.

Work Experience:
    1965-66   Year off spent temping and travelling
    1966-71 County Council   Personnel Assistant. Duties: filing,checking
                                 references,admin. payroll, junior staff welfare.
    1978-82 University   Administrative Assistant (part-time). Duties:
                                 computer records, organise graduation events,
                                 answering queries.
    1982- Chartered   Deputy Administration Officer, Graduate
    Accountants   Recruitment. Duties: Organisation of events,
                                 supervision of aptitude tests, schools liaison.
    1973-77 Voluntary Work   Playgroup Helper (part-time)
    1977-80 Local School   Parent/teacher Association.
    1991-93 Self help group   Volunteer group leader (breast cancer).

Activities and Interests: Reading, music, embroidery, travel, walking dog.

References: No.1 Current employer
                                 No.2 Counselling Course

Curriculum Vitae PATRICK STENT

Education

1987-90 College of F.E.	Certificate in Counselling (part-time)
1982 Polytechnic	MA Occupational Psychology
1978-81 University	BA Psychology (2i)

Employment

1991- Private Consultancy	Training, Psychometric Testing, Outplacement, Careers Counselling
1986-91 Commercial Firm	Training Manager
1986-87 Manufacturing Industry	Personnel Officer

Interests and Skills

A Communicator	Negotiating with Trade Union executives, addressing BPS meetings and training graduates in assertiveness have all developed my communication skills.
A Participant	As a member of school, college and town drama societies I have learned how to be a part of successful team projects.
A Reflective Practitioner	Through training courses and appraisal schemes I have learned how to give and receive constructive criticism, and to learn from mistakes.
An Enthusiast	I have always put much energy and enthusiasm into all of my activities, even those that I am not very good at such as badminton. I take calculated risks and believe that a small team can always find better ways of achieving goals than the current ones.

Activities and Interests   Drama, politics, badminton, church, travel

Personal Details

Address	D.O.B. 1941
Nationality British	Married with 3 grown-up children

After leaving school I worked for 15 years in various jobs mostly in sales. From 1974-1978, I was a Community Police Officer, achieving the rank of sergeant.

References   2 Names and addresses

Curriculum Vitae – Claire Dawn Smith

Profile
A creative, energetic and widely experienced nurse/therapist aiming for challenging senior position in hospital or community medicine. Enjoys problem-solving, prepared to take risks and prefers to work in a team. A strong believer in a multi disciplinary approach.

Address   D.O.B. 1947. Nationality

Education

1995 University Dept. of External Studies	Dip. in Counselling in Health Care Settings (BAC Accredited).	
1988 Gestalt Centre	Certificate in Gestalt	
1968 Royal College	RGN	
1965 Secondary School	6 O-Levels including Maths and English. Music Prize	

Employment

1989-94 District Hospital Behavioural Nurse/Therapist, Grade H.

Main Achievements:
* Co-pioneered successful new approaches to group work
* Major contributor to report on care in the community.
* Recruited and helped to train volunteers for working with terminally ill.
* Chaired committee for new initiatives in Care in the Community.

1983-89 Hospital. Drug and Alcohol Worker, Grade F.

Main Achievements:
* Introduced Gestalt Approach to group work.
* Presented conference paper on behavioural techniques.
* Promoted after only 2 years in the unit .
* Follow-up studies showed improved patient success rates.

1980-83 Cottage Hosp. Staff Nurse, Grade D (part-time).

1973-83 Community Care Volunteer Counsellor, ex-psychiatric patients.

1968-73 Nurse Grade B

1965-68 Student Nurse

1963-65 District Hospital Clerical work

Activities and Interests
Choir, Aerobics, Gardening, Family Outings, Tennis.

Recent Professional Training Courses	* Group Methods For Treating Depression
	* Counselling HIV Positive People
	* Advanced Counselling Skills
	* Management of Detoxification Centre
	* Training Volunteers for Hospice Work
	* Budget Management in Community Care
References	A & B

Comments

1 Jane

Unexplained gaps (1971-73) and unusual features (why four rather than three years at university?) invite negative speculation. This is the bare minimum of facts and, as her school grades are moderate, her CV is off to a poor start. She received very positive feedback from the counselling and the management courses but this is not mentioned. She does mention the dissertation but makes no link to counselling. She is actually gregarious but the stated interests look mostly solitary. In summary this is a standard, minimalist approach and is highly unlikely to have the desired effect. The excellent reference from the counselling course will probably never be seen.

2 Patrick

There is no law against leaving your personal details to the end of your CV and Patrick avoids the risk of being inappropriately stereotyped. The first item in a document has relatively greater impact so Patrick establishes his counselling/psychology credentials before the reader has the opportunity to muse over the suitability of a 'salesman' or a 'policeman' for a counselling post. I would definitely say that Patrick's maturity is an asset (he is sensitive about his age), in spite of the fact he might be working for a younger boss, and he uses both work and leisure experience to outline a well-rounded person. In summary I rather like this CV: it is certainly different to the usual 'responsibilities and duties' approach without being contrived. Patrick is one of those able characters who tends to be successful in all his varied careers.

3 Claire

This strategy aims to tell the reader about personality and ambition before going into detailed personal history and this invites immediate positive labelling by the reader. Claire decides to focus on what she feels she has achieved in the last ten years and it does not matter that Claire is not a graduate as readers of her CV will recognise that the professional qualifications and training courses are of similar status. Bullet points are quick and easy to read and Claire pays extra attention to beginnings and ends. The whole CV has a positive opening and ends with a reminder of her recent training: within each section she carefully places her best and second best items in first and last positions respectively. Because of the high value Claire places on her recent counselling diploma, she has promoted her education section ahead of her work experience. In summary I very much like this type of CV although it is only very recently that people have started to employ profile statements which invariably seem to me to work well. The very first things the reader finds out about you are the kind of person you are and where you are heading: not a bad idea don't you think?

Survey of Employers

In the first chapter I described some of the findings of my own small sample of ten employers in which I asked them direct to comment on good and bad behaviour of candidates for counselling jobs at both application and interview stages. In this particular small sample 25% of applicants failed to meet the minimum requirements of the job. Their detailed comment were as follows:–

1   **Badly Written:**
    i   Not properly addressing the person specification (5 mentions).
    ii   Poor presentation:- spelling, grammar, legibility etc. (4).
    iii   Lack of clarity (3).
    iv   Long-winded (3).
    v   Underplayed experience.
    vi   Ignored advice not to send CV.

2   **Bad at Interview:**
    i   Rambling and/or vague (5 mentions).
    ii   Failure to demonstrate the relevance of their experience and ability to do the job (4).
    iii   Answers too brief or too long (2)*.
    iv   Poor eye contact.
    v   Insufficient awareness of the equal opportunities issue in counselling.
    vi   Trying to please interviewers**.

*   Practice, expert advice, and sensitivity to the interviewers' non-verbal communication (e.g. they start to look bored if you ramble on) will help you to strike the right balance of length of replies to questions.
**   Experienced interviewers can spot this: the main give-away is the expression on the interviewee's face which signals "I am trying to work out what you want me to say and then I am going to say it".

Obviously the good practice is largely the opposite of the above.

1   **Well written:**
    i   Clearly meeting the person specification and maximizing experience (4 mentions).
    ii   Neat, well laid out and accurate spelling etc (3).
    iii   Brief, succinct and clear (3).
    iv   Enthusiasm.
    v   Willingness to learn and train.
    vi   Honesty.

2   **Good interview:**
    i   Knowledge and skills relevant to the person spec. (3 mentions).
    ii   Listening to the questions and answering to the point (3).

iii   Self awareness including how to compensate for any lack of knowledge or experience (2).

iv   Able to develop ideas creatively.

v   Moderate length answers.

vi   Succinct.

vii   Confidence.

viii   Enthusiasm.

ix   Presentation skills.

x   Smiling, good sense of humour.

"Be positive, be interesting, be yourself"

One Interviewer's Perspective

1 Some counsellors insist on genuineness, or simply being themselves at all times. This can result in dressing too informally and coming across as not eager enough.

2 Often interviewees fail to prepare and arrive not having even read the organisation's literature and not having any intelligent questions to ask.

3 Some counsellors are, and come across as, rather ponderous and other-worldly.

4 Some go 'over the top' and come across as insincerely trying to impress.

5 Some, in their genuineness, disclose too many self doubts or negative reasons for wanting the job, such as being very unhappy in their current job and/or desperate to make a change.

6 Often the employer is simply looking for a 'best fit' with existing staff or organisational needs and therefore has a certain person profile in mind. In this case you cannot guess at what is needed unless, perhaps, you ask directly.

7 It is always worth being positive even you don't get the job because, firstly, you may still be offered it if the first choice turns it down and, secondly, counselling is a 'small world' and people often know each other.

Examples of assumptions employers, perhaps unfairly, make about candidates include:–

1   Over-qualified for a job and would therefore soon get bored.

2 Over-qualified and therefore too academic and not a practitioner.

3 Apparently no publications and therefore unsuitable for a lecturing post.

4 Obviously works in a, say, cognitive-behavioural way in a department made up of psychodynamic counsellors.

If you think there is a danger of employers making a wrong assumption then you can provide the appropriate 'antidote': for example

"You might feel that I am over qualified for this post but . . ." Of course we all make mistakes, and hopefully we learn from those mistakes, but I have never, ever experienced a selection procedure where 'negative' information volunteered by candidates helped in any way. If the selectors unearth some negative information about you then so be it: it is not your job to draw attention to it. In my view your task when this occurs is to steer the information back to the positive. For example-

"Yes I accept that I under-achieved at school but my motivation for professional training has been really good as you can see by my results".

Being Selective

Every single issue can be discussed and every single question can be answered positively or negatively. The selectors are not mind-readers and so they only know what you (and eventually your referees) choose to tell them. If you go carefully back over your

"What do I feel really good about?"

experience at work and college and ask yourself the question 'what do I feel really good about?' and 'when did I get very positive feedback'? then you can more easily identify your achievements. It's surprising how much you forget and colleagues can be very helpful with some prompts. I have even met good candidates who forgot to mention a high grading in a formal appraisal by their employer. Where there is stiff competition for jobs, being positive about yourself is an essential requirement. The selection of what exactly to tell them is yours and I strongly recommend that you interpret the applications and interview process as an opportunity to make positive statements.

When in doubt you have nothing to lose by asking the employers for their guidance and I am reminded of the case of a well-known academic counsellor/practitioner who was unluckily made redundant. He was nearly always getting short-listed but was never offered the job. He had listened to a great deal of useful advice, especially about being positive at interview, and was at a loss as to what to do next. He finally plucked up courage and asked for some constructive feedback from the next employer to turn him down. This kindly employer said it was simple: he came over as very arrogant. Thinking that he was simply displaying confidence, he had unwittingly gone 'over the top'. It was largely the non-verbal communication that was seriously letting him down, which, as you will probably know, is regarded as the more authentic aspect of communication. Armed with this insider information he changed his style and was successful at the very next attempt. It is not a straightforward task to strike the right balance in applications and interviews, and expert advice, for example in a mock interview, is well worth seeking.

Useful publications that will help you to put your reserve on the back burner and make the most of your experience and qualifications include *How to Write a CV* (ULCAS, 1996), *Applications and Interviews* (King et al., 1995). Books which help you to consider the issue of career choice and change in a creative and positive way are *Assessing Your Career: Time for Change?* (Ball 1996), *Build Your Own Rainbow* (Hopson and Scally, 1993) and *What Colour Is Your Parachute?* (Bolles, 1997) although the latter is too American in style for some tastes. A new series by Chris Phillips (1996) from career choice to selection centres looks lively and useful. Your nearest university careers service will have all the above, lots more information, and may offer you other services. For creative and highly professional advice on your own CV and applications I can recommend RPR Associates, Church Walk, Combe, Witney, Oxon. OX8 8NQ (tel. 01993 898430).

Creative Jobhunting

Phillips (1988) identifies four major reasons why you might adopt a direct approach to employers.

1 Not all jobs are advertised. The reluctance to advertise, especially nationally, is that they may be deluged with applications.

2 Some employers don't realise that they need *you*. I recall one student services director of a large midlands university who realised when she received a speculative application that she badly needed to lighten her caseload. She persuaded her line manager to create a temporary post .

3 The job you want hasn't been invented yet. There may be general practices out there who would welcome some versatile person who can run a well woman clinic, with stress management and quit smoking techniques built in options.

4 You are not keen on filling in application forms. There is no law against approaching employers direct and they might well admire your initiative.

"quit smoking"

Networking is a process in which you identify and then contact people who might be helpful in your career development or job search. These include people of power and influence and also those who are doing the very job that you have in mind. Interviewing them or, better still, job shadowing them could provide you with good quality information as it is coming from the 'inside track'. Some people are born and/or educated into useful networks: for example I have noticed how confident some former pupils of famous public schools are about their chances of getting work in 'the City'. Most of us are from more humble backgrounds and may have to build our networks up from scratch, but there is no need to be bashful about using friends, relations and acquaintances. As Phillips (1988: 34) put it:-

"You'll be surprised at how readily most people will give you a little of their time"

Part of the reason is that most people enjoy talking about themselves and their careers: ask for 15 minutes and they will probably give you 45. If you have experienced assertiveness training then you will realise how techniques such as 'broken record' ("I really am very keen to talk to you") and a counselling response ("I realise you are very busy but" . . .) can help you to be pleasantly persistent.

Up to the turn of the century there is likely to be modest overall growth in counselling jobs, with more rapid increase in medical and work settings. Once you have decided exactly what job you would like to be offered, then you can plan your life in such a way as to acquire the necessary experience and training. If you are not already doing so, I suggest that you systematically monitor and evaluate your counselling and related work so that you are aware of your strengths and weaknesses and gain insight into how to improve you performance. I know that this will be anathema to some readers, especially those who prefer to consider the work of counselling to remain something of a mystery, but certainly in employment the value of this evaluation will need to be demonstrably clear and perhaps also in the case of private practice. Evaluation should ideally involve your supervisor and/or mentor and be based primarily on client feedback.

A Counselling Professional?

If counselling is to take its place alongside more established caring professions, as I hope it will, then it will have to have a clear system of individual accreditation, disciplinary procedures and a network of accredited courses. Employers are increasingly likely to require *actual* BAC or UKCP accreditation rather than its 'equivalent', and if you are fortunate yours might contribute towards the £5,000-£6,000 it will cost to obtain this qualification. In areas of the UK where there is overprovision of counselling training then the weaker/unrecognised courses are likely to disappear. Similarly where there are too many freshly trained counsellors flooding the counselling market, then this will tend to drive down fees and salaries. Thus will counselling be subject to the constraints of supply and demand, and some of you will surprise yourselves by developing marketing skills and entrepreneurial flair. Of one thing we can be sure, there will be plenty of good work to be done even if it does involve an army of part time and volunteer counsellors. As my case studies demonstrate so convincingly, there is no such person as a typical counsellor, just a fascinating variety of people each with a unique portfolio of life and work. Be positive about it.

I admit to a certain ambivalence about careers in counselling. That was my attitude when I first started work on the book, back in the autumn of 1994 and, in spite of all that I have learnt, I still feel the same way. My ambivalence springs from three main sources. Firstly, the best counselling I personally received during a two month spell in hospital came from nurses and others who had had little or no formal training. Secondly, I have encountered many students on foundation courses (and a few beyond) who are still at an 'anxious client' stage in their personal development. Thirdly, my heart sometimes sinks when I hear on the news that an army of counsellors have been sent in to the latest tragedy or disaster zone. There are too many half trained (and even outright charlatans) out there who are capable of doing more harm than good. On balance, and in spite of being an instinctive libertarian, I feel that there is a strong case for regulation. I think counselling should become a profession.

My Case Studies

My case studies and 'days in the life of' professional counsellors were not chosen at random. I have argued that there is no stereotype counsellor but I have deliberately chosen people who have been relatively successful in their counselling careers. In trying to strike the right balanace between optimism and realism, I may have tipped the scales in favour of the former. Those whose private practices have sadly failed are not represented in my book. Those whose counselling careers have stumbled because they were not emotionally robust enough, or were temperamentally unsuited to counselling in some way, or who were very unlucky, are not adequately represented in my book. On the other hand, I wanted you to listen to the advice of those who are doing well. Yes, I did say advice: those of you on person centred training courses may be in a mild state of paranoia about giving advice or in the slightest way of 'leading the client'. However, this is a book of careers guidance about counselling and I have no qualms about offering information and advice when appropriate. Of course, if you were to engage with me personally, in a careers couselling session, about your decisions about counselling as a career, then I would not dream of advising you what to do!

Stay and Hope or Move On?

In a human resources 'talking shop' recently (P-E International) it was suggested that as many as 80% of employers are now prepared to provide training and other opportunities for their staff to develop themselves, and offer interesting challenges, but not a 'job for life'. In other words, they will help you to remain 'employable'. However, only 12% of employees were described as being prepared to take more responsibility for becoming and remaining employable, so presumably the penny has yet to drop for 88%. I have argued that the distinction between public and private sectors is becoming increasingly blurred and this applies to counselling. Regardlless of how progressive or otherwise your employer is, why not take charge of your personal and professional development? Let the penny drop.

In the employed sector you will be working in partnerships to deliver your individual career objectives, for an employer whose has to realise departmental targets. The key is communication of direction of business, where the business is going, and how can you, the employees, contribute. We may have seen the worst of the cut-backs in the early 1990s. Those who survived 'downsizing', especially middle managers, may now be inclined to do nothing, but I personally can't see the rate of change going down. Watch out for 'Beyond the CV' by Helen Vandevelde (Butterworth Heinemann, forthcoming) and start thinking of replacing your CV with a 'digital portfolio'. If we cannot adapt to change then we are likely to be left behind. If, like me you want to work free-lance, it will still be helpful to engage in career path mapping and that includes action planning.

Action Planning

I have worked on this book throughout with students of counselling in mind, almost as if you were taking the careers module at Oxford Brookes University. In that module, the first of its kind in the UK, students address five questions:–

1 How do people choose careers or do careers choose them?
2 How am I going to choose a career?

3 To which careers am I best suited?
4 Which of those careers shall I investigate in detail?
5 How shall I implement my career choice?

Students are invited to draw up an action plan so that their career choice, such as counselling, does not remain a mere fantasy. My fondness for action planning dates back to my first career as a planner, from which it comes naturally to me to anticipate possible desirable futures and then to work back to the necessary decision making processes in order to translate, as far as possible, forecast into reality.

Your values are the motor that derives the action planning process, and that desire to help people in distress is probably what brought you in the first place to consider counselling as a career. Your awareness of your skills, achievements, experience and knowledge will inform career decision making and a qualified career counsellor can help you to clarify these. Values can thus be translated into broad goals.

From this process you can identify short, medium and long term objectives. These are more concrete statements which spell out, step by step, how to achieve your goals. It is often helpful to describe those objectives in terms of quantifiable targets.

Example:
Goal:– long term full time private practice.
Objectives:–
1 Complete advanced diploma by summer 1998.
2 Do voluntary work with either Relate or Drug Advisory Centre or both (by summer 1999).
3 Network with established, psychodynamic private practitioners, immediately.
4 Conduct postal questionnaire survey of large general practices in order to establish scope for referrals, by winter 1998.
5 Obtain details of short training courses in brief counselling, and buy Colin Feltham's book on the subject immediately.
6 Wait until your partner is in an exceptionally good mood, and has signalled his or her support for balanced lives in general and downshifting in particular. Then explain your plans. Get him or her on your side. Do that as soon as possible.

Counselling is, outwardly, a passive, mysterious, and subtle process. By comparison starting, maintaining and developing your career in counselling is an active, positive, unmysterious, risky, creative and exciting process. So why not get on with it? Good luck.

APPENDIX 1:
COUNSELLING IN SPORT AND ENTERTAINMENT

Introduction

Sport and entertainment are almost certainly the fastest growing and most lucrative settings for the emerging profession of counselling. Unfortunately there is a dearth of coherent data and the work is characterized by opposite ends of the spectrum— conducted either in a blaze of publicity or shrouded in secrecy, according to the public relations needs of the clients, their agents and their employers. For some famous actresses such as Andie Mc Dowell counselling or therapy is as normal and regular an activity as working out. "Of course I look after my mind as carefully as I look after my body" she said recently, visibly irritated that the interviewer should regard this as at all odd. Jokes about therapy, especially in the setting of New York, are legion, and it is sometimes difficult to take the subject really seriously. When asked how was the therapy going Woody Allen, allegedly in analysis for 27 years, once replied "slowly".

Whilst British practice seems to have been most strongly influenced by the American tradition in counselling in entertainment, in sport the overwhelming influence is European, perhaps reflecting the indifference of European culture for the sports of American football and baseball. The Dutch psychologist Aaron Thom (1996) wrote, arguably, the seminal work on football and the yob culture within the wider European context. Following some of the pioneering research techniques developed by British sociologists, Thom achieved some fame, and a touch of notoriety, when he himself needed extensive counselling to overcome the neurosis he suffered after immersing himself into the violent sub-culture of fanatical Rotterdam fans. The Norwegian counselling psychologist Sven Dikke (1997) by contrast showed some fascinating insight into the bereavement process of groups of supporters of teams relegated to lower divisions. More research in the British context is sorely needed here.

The most influential research into counselling sportsmen and women at the highest level has come from the German-American Arnold Hary (1995). Until his research attention and resources had been focused on the psychology of *performance* and Hary himself had enjoyed a highly successful career in the former GDR before retraining in counselling and working more with competitors who had gone through the pain barrier in more than the physical sense. Although it is very difficult to measure, there is anecdotal evidence to suggest that amateur sportspersons, actors and musicians are turning in increasing numbers to counselling. Increasingly leisure centre attendants and directors of top amateur operatic societies are expected to have counselling training at least to foundation level, and after spectacular defeats in sport or flops on stage, small teams may be sent in to offer post-traumatic stress counselling to members of the 'chorus'. Intensive one-to-one counselling is routinely offered to principles who have been given bad revues.

Spectacular defeats in sport

A Day in the Life of Sports Counsellor, Melvin (45)

I decided to specialise on counselling in sport partly as a result of a chance conversation with a counsellor friend of mine, Dr Wendy Dreardon. A keen Arsenal supporter in the 1970s she had once analysed a game in which Alan Hudson, the midfield player, never once passed the ball to Malcolm MacDonald the striker. She suggested to a bemused Arsenal manager Terry Neill (this personality clash was a club secret) that she be taken on as club psychotherapist but he politely declined. A keen footballer and golfer myself, I suddenly saw the possibilities.

After years of trying to fit my clients into the standard one hour slots I now operate with approximately 90 minute sessions, a regime that seems to suit me well. Sessions have a natural life af anywhere between 75 and 110 minutes, my strict upper limit. I charge clients for 90 minutes at rates ranging from £20 to £200 according to their means, and will occasionally see a client free of charge. I discovered quite early in my career that some wealthy clients want a counsellor who is reassuringly expensive.

My first client is **Wayne** who I have been seeing for nearly six months without apparently much progress. Wayne is a rather sad case of a former premier division defender now playing in the second division and still suffering from a curious inclination to score own goals, sometimes of a quite spectacular nature. He had admitted in an early session, albeit with great embarrassment, that he sometimes experienced a strange sense of exhilaration when he put into his own net. Whenever I steered the conversation to his childhood he always spoke in glowing terms about his father who he idolised. It was his father who had taught him to play and they were always described as a 'brilliant team'. I asked him gently if there was ever a time when their relationship had been difficult: after a long pause Wayne suddenly burst into floods of tears. Between sobs he described how his father had always criticised and even humiliated him if he did not perform up to scratch, but only when there was nobody else around. In public his father, a former international goalkeeper, was all smiles and full of praise, pride and encouragement. What better way to get back at his father than to score spectacular own goals? By the end of the session Wayne, who had only ever played in a defensive role on his father's insistence, was talking excitedly about the possibility of converting to midfield. As with many of my clients the flexibility of the 90 minute session enables me to wind the session down by more casual conversation. Wayne is extremely good looking and a favourite with many female fans, so we discuss the possibility of a change of hairstyle as well as team role.

My second client of the day, **Dr Hul**, is a complex character who presents an intellectual, emotional and financial challenge. A fanatical amateur golfer of moderate standard (handicap 15) he has already been twice in trouble with previous golf clubs over alleged 'banditry'. This is where a golfer is accused of deliberately playing badly in order to get their handicap put up, only then to suddenly play well in an important strokeplay tournament much to the chagrin of the opposition. I have the added complication that Dr Hul, a highly paid chartered accountant and respected expert on advanced work performance indicators, is insisting on a complex formula for my own fees.

We concentrate on his current problem, the dreaded putting 'yips'. For the benefit on non-golfers this is a very stressful affliction, which even some top players (including Bernhard Langer) have suffered from. It typically results in a tremor setting in, resulting in missed putts under three feet in length. I set up the indoor putting equipment on the carpet and I work with Dr Hul on mental imagery that should cure the affliction. Clients range from those who benefit from 'distractive' imagery, often of a sexual nature (especially with golfers and snooker players), which takes their mind off the stressful task of holing a three foot putt, and those who prefer to channel their aggression into fiercely concentrating on the task. I am not surprised that Dr Hul opts for the latter approach and settles for imagining that he is focusing the sights of his 'telescopic rifle' on the foreheads of his business rivals and golfing opponents. His hands and wrists freeze and the putt rattles satisfyingly into the artificial hole on the carpet. He punches the air in satisfaction. After some more casual conversation about his tendency to slice his metal wood tee shots at long short holes Dr Hul departs a happier man.

After lunch and a few business calls I set off for a group therapy session at a London football club's supporters association. I have only recently completed an advanced training course in group work but realise the importance of putting on a calm, confident and concerned manner. I feel a twinge of guilt that this particular club which, in my view, play a style of football frankly suited to the lower division. I do not find it difficult to facilitate discussion as the fans express their derision of the manager, (recently sacked), and hatred for Kevin, the star player who committed the sin of signing for nearby premier division rivals in mid season. I thought for one awful moment that one of the more emotional fans was going to lead us in a chorus of 'You'll Never Walk Alone', or even worse, that a dedicated vicar/fan was going to lead us in prayer, but conversation steered around to the inevitable question of choice of new manager. Paul Gascoingne and Chris Waddle as player-managers were the favourites. I sensed the optimism for the new season already beginning to bubble. Hope conquers all.

I end my day with a vigorous game of squash and imagine it is Dr. Puthindi Hul's golfball I am smashing into the wall. A quiet pint and a visit to a chamber concert with my girlfriend ends a well balanced day.

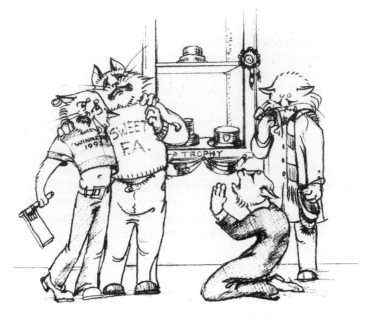

Bereavement counselling

A Week in the Life of a Luvvies Counsellor, Lucie (45)

It was my Gestalt therapist who first suggested I would be good at counselling and, after a training course modelled on the work of Melanie Hook (1994), she was kind enough to let me assist in her group until I was ready to fly solo. It was my best friend and fellow actress Gloria who suggested I should practice under the name of Lucie Loquette.

Monday. I dread Mondays in the sense that this is where I deliberately do my most difficult and unfulfilling work. I see my richest clients on Mondays and have a strict policy of seeing a maximum of two: as I charge them £100 to £300 per session I can easily afford this luxury. I have found the research work of Line (1995) on dealing with the most rich and demanding clients very reassuring.

 Diana is my only client today as Boris has cancelled at the last minute. Diana is a very successful actress and singer who is nevertheless deeply unsatisfied with her lot. Severely perfectionistic in both her work and her relationships inevitably takes a heavy toll but, like most luvvies, she enjoys the undivided attention of her counsellor. I confess that sometimes I am faking this because, when she is banging on about some part or other in a film she should have been offered, I find my mind wandering off ("must remember to get more cat litter"). Diana, who is extremely beautiful with big brown eyes, is invariably cast as the love interest in action movies, or plays the tragic heroine in weepies. Unfortunately she is a very poor judge of scripts and the last weepy I saw her in was so badly written that I ended up in hysterics and had to leave the cinema. Always finding it difficult to maintain my 'genuineness' in counselling I have become expert in oblique understatement. I told her that I wept profusely at this particular film and her eyes moistened with pleasure.

She really wants to play tragic Queens of England, or indeed any country that would have her (Bergman's Sweden perhaps?), but is patently unsuited. She asks my opinion about her chances of playing the young Elizabeth II in the forthcoming BBC 2 drama documentary. She is, of course, hopelessly unsuited and I am required to make a heroic effort to respond empathically. "It will be a character acting challenge of immense proportions. It would be truly remarkable if you could pull it off", I tell her and she glows with pride. My Gestalt training does enable me to have some fun in helping Diana to devise creative ways of preparing her for the doomed audition, such as role play conversations with imaginary royals.

I always feel guilty about Diana but she insists that our work together is vitally important and 'perception is all'. Monday and Tuesday lunchtimes I work in 'The Furkin' pub which is a great antidote to counselling the rich and famous. Lots of my acting friends, most of them 'resting', frequent this pub so it is a good chance to catch up on the gossip. A few of them know about my counselling work, but are very discrete about it.

On Tuesday I agree to see **Benjamin** (45) and **Gwendolene** (43) at short notice. They are playing in a revival of 'The Pajama Game' which is not having a good run after receiving mixed revues. Personally I was very impressed with both their performances as the warring lovers Sid and Babe but it is a very dated show (I mean, who would want to see a musical about industrial relations, other than Arthur Scargill or Tony Benn?). They are both in quite a state about the performance of fellow actor Humphrey (Babe's dad) who is an alcoholic. Now there is nothing unusual about heavy drinking in the professional theatre but Humphrey has been behaving even more erratically than usual. The session operates on three levels of which coping with the alcoholic Humphrey is the most straightforward. Ben who, struggling in his career, is seriously thinking of quitting, having become increasingly accident prone himself. I recommend a careers counsellor to him. I sense that there is more and soon the news tumbles out which explains why their performances in the musical have been so convincing: Ben and Gwendlolene have fallen in love. Without the theatre, tennis clubs and Young Conservative Associations I am sure the divorce rate in Britain would be in single figures! We talk it through.

On Wednesday and Thursday I see mostly regular clients including two from the cast of 'Eastenders' who are worried about their personalities merging with those of their characters who are, needless to say, pretty miserable. On Friday morning I audition myself for a TV film. I still have the bug to perform and now that I don't care so much whether or not I get the part my auditions are more relaxed. I am quite pleased with myself about this one.

Friday is partly my favourite day because of the occasional workshops I run at a drama school. My groupwork style is very loosely modelled on the pioneering work of the American Herman Zinker (1992), and my speciality is a workshop on coping with the complex lifestyle of of the semi-successful actor, a role on which I am an acknowledged expert! The developmental theorists say that fantasy careers are normally abandoned by the age of about ten but, as anybody who works in sport or the theatre can tell you, it isn't true for sportsmen and actors, many of whom never give up and some never even grow up. My favourite

"Lucy Loquette's Monday"

client is in his seventies and still hasn't given up on the idea of playing Von Trapp in 'The Sound of Music'.

Friday evening is my best part of the week when I work with amateurs (the 'Pucklebury Players') who have not given up on their fantasies. Directing was a complete revelation to me because I had always assumed that performing was both more creative and more fun. I have only recently discovered that writing is even more satisfying and my local village society are putting on my first play 'Climb Every Mountain'. If you can imagine what would happen if the South Torquay Amateur Dramatic Society were foolish enough to let Basil Fawlty (of 'Fawlty Towers' sitcom fame) direct a production of 'The Sound of Music' you will have a rough idea of how this comedy works.

On the train home from London I read an article which predicts that very soon we will have little need to leave home in the evenings. The technology will soon be available to enable us, at the flick of a switch, to watch any video, listen to any symphony concert, watch any drama etc. Upstairs our teenage children will have their own personal systems, so that there will no longer be any need for families to be together at all. What a nightmare scenario! I can't wait to get down to the village hall where we can have fun with live, home made entertainment. In my humble opinion, you just can't beat it. I have even persuaded my husband Rodger, who is a serious writer, to have a walk on part in the play, given the acute shortage of men in amateur dramatics. Directing a village society bears very little resemblance to working with professionals. Most amateurs have no interest in 'getting into their characters' about whom they display only passing interest. They display more keenness in getting to the pub before closing time. The Pucklebury Players are rather like Dad's Army with a similar age range and so rehearsals are very much in the character of 'Acorn Antiques'. We repair to the pub after rehearsal and much laughter accompanies discussion of the follow up production 'MacBeth – the Musical!'. Rodger is enjoying the break from his lonely life of writing and is looking distinctly amorous. Whereas Diana is probably tucked up alone in her mansion this could be my lucky night. I feel like a good Rodgering!

Postscript. Melvin and Lucie were asked to report on their clients six months after the above accounts.

Melvin reports that Wayne's career has undergone a renaissance and premier division clubs are queuing up for his signature. He is now an out and out striker and thoroughly enjoys scoring goals at the right end. He had a tearful reconciliation with his elderly father who now runs a pub in Pucklebury and sees a post trauma counsellor. Puthindi Hul's golf game unfortunately has gone to pieces and Melvin was furious to discover that the putting tremors (that had returned) were this time due to the large quantities of alcohol he had been consuming in a vain attempt to control his nerves for the big occasions.

Lucie still sees Diana who continues to appear to enjoy her apparently undivided attention. Diana is even more typecast than ever and is thinking of seeking solace in Bhuddism. Anyone for Bhuddist counselling? Benjamin and Gwendolene got married in the Caribbean and seem very happy. Ben is re-training to be a primary school teacher and Gwendolene is pregnant at the grand old age of 44. Rodger is now playing lead roles.

The author was pleased to receive this update on April 1st 1997.

References.

Tom, Dick and Harry. Series of articles in the European Journal of Sporting Psychological Health.
Hook, Line and Sinker. Series in the British Journal of Dramatic Mental Wellbeing.

Counselling is a serious occupation but it is vital to retain a sense of humour, and there is no harm in being a bit gullible. How far did you get through this chapter before the penny dropped?

REFERENCES AND USEFUL ADDRESSES

AGCAS, 1994,'What do Graduates Do?', Manchester, AGCAS.

Ashley, A, 1995, Counselling and Psychotherapy: Is there a Difference? A Response, Counselling, vol. 6, no. 2, May, 1995, Rugby, BAC.

Association of Graduate Recruiters (AGR), (1994), AGR Newsletter, no. 28, March 1994.

AGR, 1995, 'Skills for Graduates in the 21st Century', Cambridge, AGR.

Aveline, M, 1992, 'From Medicine to Psychotherapy', London, Whurr.

Ball, B, 1996, 'Assessing Your Career: Time for change?', Leicester, BPS Books.

Bell, E, Forthcoming, 'Counselling in Further and Higher Education', Buckingham, Open University Press.

Bolles, R, 1997, 'What Colour is your Parachute?, New York, 10 Speed Press.

Bramley, W. 'The Broad Spectrum Psychotherapist', Free Association Books Ltd. New York, 1996.

Bridges, K, and Goldberg, D, 1985, Somatic Presentation of DSM III Psychiatric Disorders in Primary Care, Journal of Psychosomatic Research, 29, 564-9.

British Association for Counselling (BAC),1995, 'Counselling and Psychotherapy Resources Directory 1996', Rugby, BAC.

British Association for Counselling, 1993, 'Membership Survey 1993', Rugby, BAC.

British Association for Counselling, 1995b, 'Training in Counselling and Psychotherapy A Directory 12th Edition', Rugby, BAC.

British Association for Counselling, 1993b, 'Guidelines for the Employment of Counsellors in General Practice', Rugby, BAC.

Burrell,I, and Levy, A, 1995, 'Office Workers Turn Violent in "Suit Wars", Sunday Times, 5 November 1995.

Careers Service trust, 1996, 'Survey of Post-graduate Courses in Counselling', Manchester, Central Services Unit (CSU).

CSU, 1994, 'The Supply of Graduates 1993-95: Trends and Predictions', Manchester, CSU.

Child, M, 1994, Looking Ahead, Counselling at Work, no. 5, Summer 1994.

Cooper, C, Sadri, G, Allison, T and Reynolds, P, 1990, Stress Counselling in the Post Office, Counselling Psychology Quarterly, vol. 3, no. 1.

CRAC, 1996,' POSTGRAD, The Directory of Graduate Studies 1996/7', London, Hobsons.

Dalrymple, J, 1995, Nightmare USA, Sunday Times Magazine, 3 September 1995: 34.

Department of Employment (DE),1993, 'Labour Market and Skill Trends 1994/5', London, DE.

Department of Health, 1993, 'The Health of the Nation', London, HMSO.

Dunn, C, 1994, Change Puts Workplace Counselling on the Agenda, Counselling at Work, Spring 1994.

Dryden, W, 'The Stresses of Counselling in Action', London, Sage.

East, P, 1995, 'Counselling in Medical Settings', Buckingham, Open University Press.
Elton-Wilson, J, 1994, 'Current Trends in Counselling Psychology', Invited Lecture for the BPS Annual Conference, March 1994.
Employee Assistance Programme, 1995, UK Standards of Practice and Professional Guidelines for Employee Assistance Programmes, London, EAPA.

Feltham, C, 1993, Making a Living as a Counsellor, in Dryden, W, 'Questions and Answers on Counselling in Action', London, Sage.
Feltham, C, 1995, 'What is Counselling?', London, Sage.
Feltham, C, 1996, 'Brief Counselling', London, Sage.

Gale, A, 1990, 'Thinking About Psychology?', BPS Books.
Galliano, S, Counsellor Criteria for EAPs, Counselling at Work, Summer 1994.
Goldberg, D, and Huxley, P, 1992, 'Common Mental Disorders: a Biosocial Model', London, Tavistock/Routledge.
Guy, J, 1987, 'The Personal Life of a Psychotherapist', New York, Wiley.

Harrison, S, 1993, 'Counselling in Four Practices in Oxfordshire: Analysis of Referrals and Patient Satisfaction', Buckinghamshire, FHSA.
Hay, D, 1987, 'Exploring Inner Space' (second edition), Oxford, Mowbray.
Hopkins, V, 1994, Is Counselling for the Organisation or the Employee?, Counselling at Work, Spring 1994.
Hopson, B, and Scally, M, 1993, 'Build Your Own Rainbow', Leeds, Lifeskills Associates.

Institute for Employment Research (IER), 1991, 'Review of the Economy and Employment: Occupational Assessment', London, IER.

King, D, Parkin, Y, and Healy, R, 1995, 'Applications and Interviews', Manchester, CSU.
Klinefelter, P, 1994, A School Counselling Service, Counselling, vol. 5 No.3, August 1994, BAC.
Krebs, R, 1980, Why Pastors should not be Counsellors, Journal of Pastoral Care, XXXIV, 4, December.
Kubler-Ross, E, 'On Death and Dying', London, Routledge.

Lightfoot, L, 1994, Trauma Brings Counsel that is not so Wise, Sunday Times, Issue 8850.
Lyall, D, 1995, 'Counselling in the Pastoral and Spiritual Context', Buckingham, Open University Press.

Macwhinnie, L, 1994, Detecting and Dealing with Depression, Counselling at Work, Spring 1994.
Mann, A, 1993, The Need for Counselling, in Corney, R, and Jenkins, R, (eds), 'Counselling in General Practice', London, Tavistock/Routledge.

McMahon, G, and Powell, K, 'Starting Your Own Private Practice: A basic Guide to Self employment', Loughton, Gale Centre Publications.

MIND, 1993, 'Policy Pack', London, MIND Publications.

Monach, J, and Monroe, S, 1993, 'An Evaluation of Counselling in General Practice: a Baseline Study of Services in Sheffield', Sheffield, Sheffield Hallam University.

Moore, S, 1995, Furthermore, *Guardian*, 24 August 1995.

Nathan, R, and Hill, L, 1994, 'Career Counselling', London, Sage.

Nayler-Smith, 1994, Counselling and Psychotherapy, Is There a Difference?, *Counselling*, November, 1994, vol. 5, no.4, Rugby, BAC.

Nelson-Jones, R, 1991, 'The Theory and Practice of Counselling Psychology', Cassell.

P-E International, 'Talking Shop Cassette', Park House, Wick Rd. Egham, Surrey.

Phillips, C, 1996, 'No Idea about Career?', 'First Interviews- sorted!', 'Second Interviews and Assessment Centres', 'Making Wizard Applications', Just the Job Handbooks, GTI/Independent.

Phillips, C, 1988, 'Creative Job Search', Newpoint.

Rajan , A, 1992, '1990s: Where will the New Jobs Be?', London, Institute of Careers Guidance.

Riddick, E et al., 'Guidance and Counselling ', Manchester, CSU.

Ross, R, AGCAS 2000 a Politically Incorrect Perspective, *Phoenix*, issue no. 63, December 1992, Manchester, CSU.

Sarler, F, 1995, 'How the Nation Loved, Laughed, Lost and Cried, then Went for Counselling', *Sunday Times Magazine*, 12 November 1995.

Sibbald,B, and Addington-Hall, J, Brennerman, D, and Freeling, 1993, 'Counsellors in English and Welsh General Practices: their Nature and Distribution, *British Medical Journal*, 306: 29-33.

Skynner, R, and Cleese, J, 1983, 'Families and How to Survive Them', London, Methuen.

Strathdee, G, and Sutherby, D, 1993, 'Literature Review for the Development of a Primary Care Strategy for Mental Health', Prism (Psychiatric Research in Service Measurement), London, Institute of Psychiatry.

Sturgeon, D, 1985, Medical Student Training: The Situation in Great Britain, in Wolff, H, Knaus, W, (eds) 'First Steps in Psychotherapy: Teaching Psychotherapy to Medical Students and General Practitioners', Berlin, Springer-Verlag.

Switzer, D, 1983, Why Pastors Should be Counsellors (of a Sort), *Journal of Pastoral Care*, XXVII, 1,March.

Syme, G, 'Counselling in Independent Practice', 1994, Buckingham, Open University Press.

Thoburn, M, August 1995, 'Information for Counsellors and Counselling Organizations', UKRC, Rugby, BAC.

Thomas, R, and Corney, R, 1993, Working with Community Health Officials: a Survey Among General Practitioners, *British Journal of General Practice*, 43 (375): 417-21.

Tyndall, N, 1993, 'Counselling in the Voluntary Sector', Buckingham, Open University Press.

University of London Careers Advisory Service (ULCAS), 1995, 'How to Write a CV', London, ULCAS.

Vandevelde, H, (forthcoming), 'Beyond the CV: Securing a lifetime of work in the global marketplace', Oxford, Butterworth Heinemann.

Watts, A, 1994, 'Lifelong Career Development', Occasional Paper, Cambridge, CRAC.

Watts, A, 1995, In My View, *Insight*, vol. 3 no. 33, NICEC.

Watts, M and Bor, R, 1995, 'Professional Psychology Handbook', BPS Books.

Wavell, S, When is a Story Unhealthy?, *Sunday Times News Review*, 15 October 1995: 3.

White, L, 1997, Speaking Your Mind, *Sunday Times Magazine*, 5 January 1997, London.

Wood, D, 1993, Wordswordswordswords: the Power of Words: Uses and Abuses of Talking Treatments', London, MIND Publications.

Useful Names and Addresses

Advice, Guidance, Counselling and Psychotherapy Lead Body (AGC&PLB),
40A, High St.
Welwyn,
Herts. AL6 9EQ.

Association of Graduate Careers Advisory Services (AGCAS), and Central Services Unit (CSU),
Crawford House,
Precinct Centre,
Manchester, M13 9EP.

Association of Graduate Recruiters (AGR),
Sheraton House,
Castle Park,
Cambridge, CB3 0AX.

British Association for Counselling (BAC),
1 Regents Place,
Rugby
Warwickshire, CV21 2PJ.

CEPEC,
67, Jermyn St.
London SE1 6NY.

Counselling in Primary Care Trust,
Suite 3a,
Majestic House,
High St.
Staines, TW18 4DG.

EAP Association,
Wyvols Court,
Swallowfield,
Reading,
Berkshjre RG7 1PY.

FOCUS,
Northside House,
Mount Pleasant,
Barnet,
Herts, EN4 9EB.

MIND,
National Association for Mental Health,
22 Harley St.
London W1N 2ED/

United Kingdom Council for Psychotherapy (UKCP),
Regent's College,
Inner Circle,
Regent's Park,
London NW1 4NS.